Towards an Integrated Health Information System in the Netherlands

OECD

BETTER POLICIES FOR BETTER LIVES

This work is published under the responsibility of the Secretary-General of the OECD. The opinions expressed and arguments employed herein do not necessarily reflect the official views of the Members of the OECD.

This document, as well as any data and map included herein, are without prejudice to the status of or sovereignty over any territory, to the delimitation of international frontiers and boundaries and to the name of any territory, city or area.

The statistical data for Israel are supplied by and under the responsibility of the relevant Israeli authorities. The use of such data by the OECD is without prejudice to the status of the Golan Heights, East Jerusalem and Israeli settlements in the West Bank under the terms of international law.

Please cite this publication as:
OECD (2022), *Towards an Integrated Health Information System in the Netherlands*, OECD Publishing, Paris, https://doi.org/10.1787/a1568975-en.

ISBN 978-92-64-83436-1 (print)
ISBN 978-92-64-70158-8 (pdf)

Foreword

OECD countries are increasingly concerned with having the right data infrastructure in place for producing health statistics and measuring health care quality and outcomes. This relates to information gathered through registries, administrative data, EHRs, and other sources – and concerns data linkage between settings and levels of care, and mechanisms to generate and use timely, actionable data. Interest in strengthening health information systems has grown since the COVID-19 pandemic has brought into sharp focus the importance of reliable, up-to-date information for decision making.

The OECD launched country reviews of health information systems in January 2021 to support countries in developing health information systems for the digital age. Country reviews follow a method where OECD and national experts jointly undertake a process of uncovering the barriers and facilitators to each country's progress toward a 21st Century health information system. With a common core of content, the reviews can be compared across participating countries, furthering the value of the project to all countries.

The framework for the evaluation of each health information system is the OECD Council Recommendation on Health Data Governance which calls for National Health Data Governance Frameworks and sets out the key principles of such frameworks. All countries are encouraged to adhere to this Recommendation which provides guidance for building national governance frameworks that enable personal health data to be both protected and used towards public policy goals. The Recommendation:

- Encourages the availability and use of personal health data, to the extent that this enables significant improvements in health, health care quality and performance and, thereby, the development of healthy societies while, at the same time, continuing to promote and protect the fundamental values of privacy and individual liberties;
- Promotes the use of personal health data for health-related public policy objectives, while maintaining public trust and confidence that any risks to privacy and security are minimised and appropriately managed; and
- Supports greater harmonisation among the health data governance frameworks of Adherents so that more countries can benefit from statistical and research uses of data in which there is a public interest, and so that more countries can participate in multi-country statistical and research projects, while protecting privacy and data security.

The first country review undertaken was of the health information infrastructure of the Netherlands in 2021. The Netherlands' Ministry of Health, Welfare and Sport commissioned the review to support the country in reforming a fragmented data landscape into an integrated health information system that would meet the needs of Dutch society in the digital age. This review supports the Netherlands as it embarks on reforms to safely use health data to power integrated, patient-centred, services and foster medical and health R&D.

Acknowledgements

This report is part of a series of country reviews of health information systems that was launched by the OECD Working Party on Health Care Quality and Outcomes (HCQO) and is part of the 2021/22 programme of work of the OECD Health Committee. The OECD thanks the experts within the Netherlands that gave of their time to participate in interviews and focus groups. The OECD acknowledges Herko Coomans for his support in co-ordinating the study in the Netherlands. The report was authored by Jillian Oderkirk, Luke Slawomirski and Véronique Bos with input and guidance from Niek Klazinga and David Morgan, and assistance from Ricardo Sanchez Torres. Thanks are extended to Francesca Colombo and Frederico Guanais for their comments on a preliminary draft.

Table of contents

FIGURES

TABLES

Follow OECD Publications on:

http://twitter.com/OECD_Pubs

http://www.facebook.com/OECDPublications

http://www.linkedin.com/groups/OECD-Publications-4645871

http://www.youtube.com/oecdilibrary

OECD http://www.oecd.org/oecddirect/
Alerts

Executive summary

Twenty-first century health systems have to be built around data and information. An integrated health information system enables the secure exchange and flow of data to where they can be used to create information and knowledge that advances policy objectives. In the Netherlands, an integrated health information system is needed to support developing, delivering and monitoring integrated health care delivery; offering integrated public health monitoring and management, including of the COVID-19 pandemic; capitalising on recent innovations in health information; and fostering research and innovation in technologies and treatments that improve health and health care.

A range of data assets is relevant for these policy objectives. This includes data generated during acute- and long-term health care and data on public health and social care. The integrated health information system should cover the health system as a whole, as well as on other relevant data sources such as social, economic and environmental data.

Countries making progress toward an integrated health information system appreciate that data are a non-rivalrous asset and that each data point can and should have many uses. Data have many of the features of a public good, and should be harnessed to generate maximum social benefit. To do this, all data must be coded according to agreed technical and semantic formats. It is only in this way that data can be meaningfully exchanged, sent to where they are needed, or analysed.

The OECD reviewed the health information infrastructure in the Netherlands using the OECD Council Recommendation on Health Data Governance as the analytical framework. It drew information from interviews and focus groups with Dutch experts from academia, business, and government and from OECD and other surveys and reports monitoring health data development, use and governance.

This report describes the requirements and the benefits of an integrated health information system; outlines the current situation in the Netherlands in the context of progress across OECD countries; and recommends legal, policy and operational changes to overcome barriers to the efficient exchange and sharing of health data and to establish an integrated health information system.

Challenges and opportunities of the 21st Century require a new approach

The Dutch health system has many strengths that can be harnessed to develop a world-class health data infrastructure and information system, including strong patient engagement and leadership of patient groups toward data interoperability; progress in developing data exchange standards; universities and institutions that are leading good practice in common data models and technologies enabling large-scale research on distributed data; and a unique 'can-do' culture.

However, the Dutch system also has several fundamental barriers that need to be overcome. One of these is health system fragmentation, a design feature that enables competition and market mechanisms to work but also presents an institutional barrier to data sharing and exchange. Fragmentation has particularly affected electronic medical data, where despite efforts toward data exchange, the data remain underdeveloped, siloed and underused. Lack of alignment and a common interpretation of legislation and regulations also present a challenge to advancing secure health data sharing, accessibility and use. Overall, this review found that while there are many strong organisations developing data in silos, there are few incentives from government or from the private sector to integrate the silos into a whole health information system.

The Dutch health system has served the country very well in the 20th century. But the challenges and opportunities of the 21st century are different, and the increasing quantity of generated health data call for a political choice, legislative guidance and fitting strategic action in order to facilitate ethical and optimal use of this rapidly expanding resource.

Creating an integrated health information system that meets the needs and opportunities of the 21st century will require a unified national strategy and a new set of institutional functions to develop, implement and oversee a health data infrastructure and integrated information system. Successful implementation will require good governance that builds trust among all stakeholders.

Development of a national strategy toward an integrated health information system

The *Ministerie van Volksgezondheid, Welzijn en Sport* would lead the development of a National Strategy in the form of a strategic plan that considers the data assets and information infrastructure already in place and builds forward from them. Developing the plan requires working with stakeholders to determine the objectives of the strategy and the values that the stakeholders want to uphold.

It is essential that the strategy is sufficiently broad and deep. Breadth refers to incorporating the four main data types: health care, public health, social care and long-term care data. Depth ensures that all data are included, and that they can be linked at the individual level to enable better care integration as well as more precision and scope in secondary uses. An important accompaniment to the digital strategy is a set of roadmaps for each strategic objective, particularly those that will be challenging to achieve, such as data interoperability.

To lead the development of the national strategy it is recommended that the Ministry:

- Builds trust and support for the strategy through consultation with governmental and non-governmental stakeholders on needs for information, analytics and information products.
- Builds public trust through a public information campaign, public consultations and other avenues in order to include inputs from the public into the strategy and provide a website to share information about the development process and its outcome.
- Considers developing a broad digital strategy encompassing the health data strategy and ensuring full alignment.
- Develops the draft high-level IT architecture/infrastructure for an integrated health information system that meets the information needs of key stakeholders, including global standards for data exchange and semantic interoperability, privacy-by-design protections and interoperability in analytics, information and knowledge.
- Develops the policy tools and financial incentives to realise the strategy.

It is also recommended that the ministry further develop and strengthen the national health data governance legislative framework to support the national strategy. The framework should specify how to ensure uniform data and interoperability standards, enable the exchange, access to and use of data to serve the health-related public interest, support 'privacy by design', and align with EU regulations.

A national agency to implement and oversee the health information system

A single agency will be needed to co-develop and implement the national strategy with the ministry and to oversee and maintain the resulting integrated health information system. This could be done by 'strengthening' or combining expertise of existing organisations or creating a new agency.

It is recommended that the ministry develop the role and legal mandate to launch the agency and to ensure that the governance of the agency provides a formal involvement of key stakeholders in the health information system.

It is recommended that the national agency take responsibility for four key activities that are essential for an integrated health information system:

1) Agreeing (or developing) and maintaining consistent **national standards** for terminology (semantics), data exchange (electronic messaging), analytics, data accessibility and sharing and harmonisation of data privacy and security policies and practices.

2) **Certification** including for vendors of IT solutions and digital tools for compliance with national standards; and verifying through quality checks and audits that health care providers and other information system actors have achieved interoperability standards and are exchanging useable (quality) data and are not blocking data flow.

3) Building and maintaining a national **public data platform** for public data exchange, acting as a hub through which the data flows. The platform should enable effective and secure processing of personal health data including data integration/linkage; foster adoption of a common health data model (CDM); manage the approval process for data integration and access requests involving data from multiple organisations; enable effective and secure mechanisms for access to personal health data for approved purposes, such as approved research; improving data quality, including conducting data quality auditing; and reducing overlapping and duplicative administrative and data processing activities among key stakeholders within the health information system.

4) **Stakeholder engagement and public consultation** about the national strategy and its implementation; and **public transparency** through clear communication about the national strategy and the development, exchange, uses and data privacy and security protections of health data.

1 Key findings and recommendations

Twenty-first century health systems will be built around data and information. Their success will depend on secure exchange and movement of data to create useful information and knowledge that advance public policy objectives. This chapter brings together the key findings of this review of how health data are managed and used in the Netherlands and the recommendations for creating an integrated national health data infrastructure and health information system. The chapter outlines what is meant by health data and an integrated health information system, and its role in advancing health care, social care, long-term care, public health and biomedical science. It outlines the strengths and challenges of the Dutch health system in the context of using health data to advance the health and well-being of individuals and populations. It concludes with a summary of recommendations to establish a modern, integrated health information system in the Netherlands.

In January 2021, the Ministerie van Volksgezondheid, Welzijn en Sport of the Netherlands commissioned the OECD to gather evidence and recommend legal, policy and organisational reforms to support creating an integrated health information system to support four key national policy goals:

1. Strengthening integrated health care delivery across settings and sectors (so that an individual's relevant health information can be accessed by them as well as their providers ranging from first responders to general practitioners to hospitals and allied health providers)

2. Enabling comprehensive public health monitoring and management (including of the COVID-19 pandemic)

3. Capitalising on recent innovations in health information infrastructure

4. Fostering research and innovation in technologies and treatments that improve health and health care.

To understand the strengths and weaknesses of the current health information system and to develop recommendations, the OECD, through a series of focus groups and interviews, consulted national experts from academia, business, and government regarding the Netherlands' health information system in January to October of 2021 (See Annex A). The discussions focussed on three questions:

- Health data interoperability (exchange and sharing): What are the challenges and what are the policy tools that can address them? i.e. regulations, incentives, standards, certification?

- Personal health environment: What are the digital tools that deliver a modern health care experience, provide data access and allow interactivity?

- Organisation and governance: What national institutions and governance mechanisms support a strong and trustworthy national health information system?

The information gathered through consultations with experts was complemented with information on the Netherlands and other OECD countries collected through the OECD's regular monitoring countries' health information systems including: 1. Survey of National Health Data Development, Use and Governance (2019-20), and 2. Survey of Electronic Health Record System Development, Data Use and Governance (2021).

This is the final report and recommendations from the OECD review. The report comprises four chapters. This chapter (Chapter 1) summarises the key findings and recommendations. Chapter 2 outlines the Dutch health system with regard to how its structure, organisation and governance influence the way health and social care data are generated, managed and used to advance the four objectives listed above. It also describes the requirements and the benefits of an integrated health information system where data can be accessed efficiently and securely by actors who need them and those who can generate valuable information and knowledge by using them. It also outlines the current situation in the Netherlands in the context of progress across OECD countries. Chapter 3 examines the main strengths and shortcomings of current arrangements in the Netherlands to manage health and social care data including legislation and policies, health information infrastructure and health data interoperability. Chapter 4 outlines legal, policy and operational changes to establish an integrated health information system. It sets out the requirements to take advantage of strengths and to address the problems uncovered in this study.

An integrated health information system for the 21st century

Twenty-first century health systems will be built around data and information. In simple terms, an integrated health information system enables the secure exchange and movement of data to where they can be used to create information and knowledge that advances policy objectives. Integrated health information systems require a strong data infrastructure made up of the relevant data assets, technology, agencies and institutions needed for the collection, storage, maintenance, distribution and (re)use of data by the different end users. While infrastructure is a key element, an information system also includes the capacity to convert raw data into usable information and knowledge. A useful analogy is an integrated transportation network, which allows passengers to move safely and securely across regional boundaries around the entire country using various transport types. While the physical and technical infrastructure is an essential component, such a system also requires people and institutions to ensure it operates effectively, efficiently, and predictably.

Every data point has several potential uses

An integrated health information system would help the Netherlands directly improve care quality, outcomes and patient empowerment by enabling patients and their health care providers to access health information (primary data use). The importance of this was recently highlighted in the Dutch media,[1] which reported difficulties with transferring COVID-19 patients between hospitals because their medical information cannot be exchanged electronically. This results in not only delays and inefficiencies – with busy clinicians having to manually transcribe patients' data from the local electronic record to a CD to send with the patient – but also the risk of subsequent medical errors that manual transcribing of information entails.

An integrated health information system would also raise the country's capacity to use these data for other important purposes (secondary data use) including:

- Managing health system performance on national, regional and network levels,
- Public health monitoring and surveillance,
- Opening new communications channels with patients to improve patient-centred care such as the active use of patient-reported metrics (PROMs and PREMs),
- Introduction of new digital services such as e-prescriptions or telehealth,
- Better targeting of reimbursement for services to reward value,
- Biomedical research and development, and
- Innovation such as big data analytics and artificial intelligence that will enhance knowledge-based decisions for patient care and health system governance.

This would enable better public health policies and interventions, and health system management. It would enable biotechnology innovation and enable the Netherlands to participate in global health efforts and make the country an attractive destination for capital investment.

A range of data assets is relevant for these purposes. For the Netherlands, this implies data generated during acute- and long-term health care as well as data on public health (publieke gezondheid) and social care (sociale domein) (Figure 1.1). The integrated health information system should cover the health system as a whole as well as drawing on other relevant data sources such as social, economic and environmental data where necessary.

Figure 1.1. Four main types of data in the Netherlands

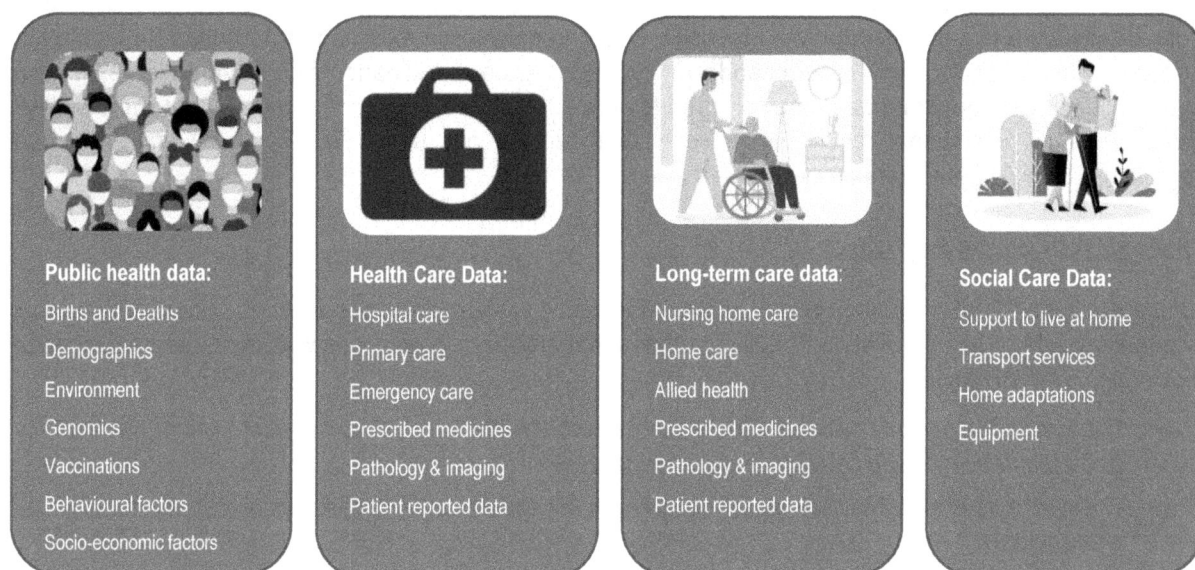

Public health data:	Health Care Data:	Long-term care data:	Social Care Data:
Births and Deaths	Hospital care	Nursing home care	Support to live at home
Demographics	Primary care	Home care	Transport services
Environment	Emergency care	Allied health	Home adaptations
Genomics	Prescribed medicines	Prescribed medicines	Equipment
Vaccinations	Pathology & imaging	Pathology & imaging	
Behavioural factors	Patient reported data	Patient reported data	
Socio-economic factors			

Image credits: © Shutterstock.com/Moab Republic, Shutterstock.com/Cube 29, Shutterstock.com/Millering, Shutterstock.com/Qualit Design.

Interoperability and governance enable efficient and secure exchange of data

Countries making progress in this regard appreciate that data are a non-rivalrous asset and that each data point can and should have many uses. Data have many of the features of a public good, and should be harnessed to generated maximum social benefit. To do this, all data must be coded according to agreed technical and semantic formats. Only this way can data be meaningfully exchanged, sent to where they are needed, or analysed. Standardisation is especially important in a highly fragmented and disaggregated health system like the Netherlands.

It is important to stress that an integrated health information system does not require all data of a certain type to be kept in a single location. It is quite possible to achieve the key objectives outlined above without central storage or even aggregation. A unified and co-ordinated approach to national data governance can enable smooth information exchange and use for a range of purposes without compromising privacy, security and ownership of data. In fact, a federated approach to data (which is more compatible with the Dutch health system's structure and governance) can be more secure.

Ensuring that data can be exchanged across national borders into Europe and beyond can amplify the benefits of data analytics and research in, for example, the context of public health, rare diseases, pharmacovigilance and precision medicine. An information system that follows international data standards facilitates within-country and cross-border health care delivery and business opportunities for the Netherland's research and technology sectors; and is better prepared to participate in and adapt to European regulations and initiatives.

For secondary uses of data (statistics and research etc.) an intermediary solution to improve health data interoperability is a **Common Data Model (CDM)**. A CDM maps data from multiple organisations that use different standards to a standardised structure that makes it possible for data to be used for analytical applications, allowing for efficient data pooling and data integration for health statistics and research. However a CDM is not a practical solution for most primary uses of data such as enabling the smooth exchange of data between health care providers for direct patient care or the development of a patient portal.

A well-designed, integrated health information system requires a data governance framework that avoids the over-use of consent to authorise data exchange, in favour of legal authorisation and an approach that protects privacy and ensures data security while enabling data to be exchanged and used for legitimate purposes. The OECD Council Recommendation on Health Data Governance sets out the elements for a national health data governance framework and fosters a 'privacy-by-design'[2] approach that is consistent with emerging transnational requirements such as those set out in the *EU General Data Protection Regulation* (GDPR) (See Annex B).

Clinical data play a key role

Clinical data are a key component of any health information system looking to improve care quality as well as enable research and innovation. OECD countries that are making progress with their integrated health information systems have:

- Established a **national organisation** that is responsible for setting national clinical terminology and electronic messaging (exchange) standards;
- Created a **multidisciplinary governing body** for the national organisation that represents key stakeholders;
- Use **unique identification** of patients and health care providers;
- Adopted **international terminology standards** for diagnoses, medications, laboratory tests and medical images;
- Adopted the **HL7 FHIR standard** for data exchange (electronic messaging); and participate in **global collaborative projects** to improve international data standards.

Most countries have one **country-wide electronic health record system** and are exchanging EHRs at the national level including data sharing among physician offices and hospitals about patients' treatment, medication use, laboratory tests and images.

Most countries have a **Patient Internet Portal** where patients can access their own medical records from all of their current health care providers. Many countries are also utilising EHRs for other secondary purposes including **public health monitoring,** health system **performance monitoring**, patient safety **surveillance** and health and medical **research**. Some are also developing **big data analytics** including machine learning, artificial intelligence algorithms with EHRs.

OECD countries have reported in a recent OECD survey several levers to improve the spread and interoperability of their electronic clinical data.

- a **legal requirement** for health care providers to meet national standards for EHR interoperability. Thirteen countries reported to have a legal requirement for health care providers to adopt an electronic health record system (software) that conformed with national standards for both clinical terminology and electronic messaging (exchange).
- a **certification of eHR system (software) vendors** that required them to adopt national standards for both clinical terminology and electronic messaging. Again, 13 have a certification that requires software vendors to meet requirements for national EHR interoperability.
- **financial incentives** (or penalties) for health care providers to install an EHR system that meets national standards and requirements for national EHR interoperability. Nine countries report incentives for health care providers to keep their EHR system up-to-date as clinical terminology and electronic messaging standards change over time; and 8 report incentives for health care providers to install and EHR system from a certified software vendor.

Building on strengths while addressing existing barriers

The Dutch health system has many strengths that can be harnessed to develop a world-class health data infrastructure and information system: strong patient engagement and leadership of patient groups toward data interoperability; progress in developing data exchange standards; Dutch universities and institutions are leading good practice in common data models and technologies enabling large-scale research on distributed data; and a unique 'can-do' culture. In the Centraal Bureau voor de Statistiek (CBS), the country has an agency with the capacity and experience in a privacy-by-design approach to data development, linkage, sharing and accessibility that is secure and privacy-protective (see Box 1.1).

However, the Dutch system also has several fundamental barriers that need to be overcome. One of these is the fragmentation – a design feature that enables competition and market mechanisms to work but that also presents an institutional block to data sharing and exchange. The current Dutch health data landscape is characterised by the highest number of data custodians reported in the OECD. This fragmented structure does not preclude being able to leverage available data to achieve the objectives listed earlier. It does, however, create greater challenges to data sharing and integration than in other countries.

Laws and regulations need to be aligned with policy objectives

Lack of alignment and a common interpretation of legislation and regulations also present a challenge. Data custodians have varying interpretations of laws and regulations such as the *EU General Data Protection Regulation* (GDPR) for example. A fragmented approach to health data management creates (a) missed opportunities to generate improvements in health and other desirable outcomes, and (b) heightened risk of personal health data being compromised. Both a national health data governance framework and guidance on the implementation of the GDPR would help to overcome different legal interpretations that are limiting data sharing in the Netherlands.

A further issue raised by experts in the Netherlands are legacy legislations that precede the GDPR and that may create unnecessary obstacles to the exchange and use of health data. In particular, the *Medical Treatment Contracts Act* (Wgbo) requires doctors to obtain patient consent to share data with third parties. Third parties include quality standards/registers. Under Wgbo, patients are required to provide explicit consent for their records to be included within the Landelijk Schakel Punt (LSP). As a result, the exchange is missing data on non-consenting patients and for patients whose health care provider did not ask them to provide consent. This limits the reliability of the data for direct care or secondary uses.

A new framework law (Wegiz) introduced in 2021 aiming to improve health data interoperability takes a cautious and incremental approach, raising concerns among experts interviewed that full health data interoperability would not be achieved in the medium term. The framework law will likely require additional follow-on administrative orders to authorise the new standards called for by professional groups. Experts interviewed are concerned that the process could be slow and potentially result in conflicting and incomplete sets of standards. However, a recent letter from Minister De Jonge to parliament (15 October 2021) outlines ways in which implementation of the Wegiz is being expedited.

The Wegiz requires that apart from the technical information standards, (addressing the how) a complementary set of clinical content oriented quality standards (addressing the what) are developed and included in the National Quality Standards Register held by Zorginstituut Nederland (ZiN). To evaluate and adopt these different types of standards seems a complex undertaking. Before recommending standards, it will be necessary to evaluate whether health care providers and organisations could conform to new requirements and the evaluation will necessitate acquiring knowledge about the various IT architectures and software in current use including the different structured terminology standards and uses of free text (unstructured data).

Box 1.1. Dutch health information infrastructures with beneficial features

While there are many health data custodians in the Netherlands, three research infrastructures have emerged whose aims and purpose align with those envisaged for the developing EU Health Data Spaces.

The Health Research Infrastructure initiative (**Health-RI**) aims to establish an interconnected data infrastructure for Dutch personalised medicine and health research. Experts interviewed indicate that Health-RI would like to access data within hospital and GP electronic health record systems for approved research projects in real time and use distributed analytics to protect privacy and data security (personal health train).

ODISSEI (Open Data Infrastructure for Social Science and Economic Innovations) provides researchers with access to the data holdings of the CBS, including the micro-data in-flowing to CBS from Dutch Hospitals, GPs, health insurers and research institutes as well as health survey data and information on the health care industry and follows 'privacy-by-design' practices to offer secure data linkage and access to data as well as advanced computing and analytics.

Netherlands leads the **EU EHDEN** (European Health Data and Evidence Network) project. Participating organisations re-code their health and clinical data to the OMOP Common Data Model. Participating organisations are part of a federated network with a 'privacy-by-design' approach where data remain at all times in the custody of the organisations holding them and network researchers submit queries and programs (distributed analytics) without accessing or visualising the personal health data. Code is shared through GitHub, supporting interoperability of data analytics as well as of data.

Source: Dutch Tech Centre for Life Sciences (2021[1]), "Health-RI", https://www.dtls.nl/large-scale-research-infrastructures/health-ri/; ODISSEI (2021[2]), https://odissei-data.nl/en/; EHDEN (2021[3]), https://www.ehden.eu/.

Many data assets are fragmented and not easily exchanged

The Dutch approach to electronic medical data is perhaps the most striking example of fragmentation. While notable initiatives such as MedMij and LSP are trying to address this, the lack of co-ordination and steering is evident. Experts interviewed described that most health care organisations have engaged software vendors to develop bespoke EHR platforms to specifications that suit their requirements and priorities. In most cases, and in the absence of an overarching national data strategy and governance framework, little attention has been paid to exchanging data. Experts described that many providers are locked into agreements with their vendors, who either limit or charge large sums to retrofit interoperability and exchange capability into their systems.

The situation is likely to continue without legislation, certification and financial incentives to prevent information blocking by software vendors and to encourage software vendors to provide modern IT architectures that support data exchange and analytical uses of data that are in the public interest. This can, in fact, create a level playing field for competition and the market to thrive while advancing public policy objectives.

Meanwhile, information standards developed by either the Nationaal ICT Instituut in de Zorg (Nictiz) or MedMij are voluntary and participation in a data exchange is voluntary. Moreover, multiple institutes are funded by the government to collect data on aspects of health or parts of the health care system. However, funding is not contingent upon collaboration among them and data interoperability among them is not required. Similarly, 'hoofdlijnakkoorden' (outline agreements) between the government and specific sectors such as medical specialists, include agreements on finances and quality but not on data interoperability. As a result, sectors continue to operate in silos. While the government provides financial incentives to physicians and hospitals to become MedMij certified; certification does not include verification that the data within MedMiJ are interoperable, nor verification that the user experience for patients would meet reasonable expectations. For example, verification of how well health information is integrated and presented to the patient is not included.

In the near term, standardisation of health data could support health care quality measurement and information by mapping/re-coding data from the diverse array of information systems in the Netherlands to a common data model (CDM). While this may not be feasible for health organisations with the most customised and irregular IT systems, it may be possible for most health care providers and organisations holding health data to have their existing data mapped/re-coded to a CDM.

Experts also raised concern about incentives. In the absence of financial incentives for data interoperability, the benefits of data interoperability and integration mainly accrue to government, researchers and health insurers; while the costs of improving the interoperability of health information systems are mainly borne by health care providers. Government leadership and legislative and policy tools are needed to create the right environment for information exchange and collaboration.

While many countries are gearing up to use data, including health data, as the fuel to power research and innovation, the Netherlands risks being left behind in this regard unless current deficiencies in data governance, interoperability and exchange are addressed. A recent Open Data Institute report put the Netherlands in the 'limited vision' category for advancing the secondary use of health data when compared with other EU countries (Boyd M, 2021[4]).

The way forward: A cohesive strategy, concerted governance, and strong leadership

The Dutch health system has served the country very well in the 20th century. But the challenges and opportunities of the 21st century are different, and the increasing quantity of generated health data calls for a political choice, legislative guidance and fitting strategic action in order to facilitate ethical and optimal use of this rapidly expanding resource.

The first thing to say is that radical overhaul of the entire health system is not required. However, creating an integrated health information system that meets the needs and opportunities of the 21st century will require a unified national strategy (preferably aligned with a broader national digital / data strategy). It will require a new set of institutional functions to develop, implement and oversee a health data infrastructure and integrated information system, either through a new national agency or by consolidating and strengthening the remit, function, and competencies of existing agencies. Successful implementation will require good governance, policy, and trust among all stakeholders.

The following is a summary of recommended actions to develop an integrated health information system in the Netherlands that are set out more fully in Chapter 4.

Develop a national strategy for an integrated health information system

The Ministerie van Volksgezondheid, Welzijn en Sport **would lead the development of a National Strategy** in the form of a **strategic plan** that considers the data assets and information infrastructure already in place and builds forward from them to develop the tracks and signals that are missing. Developing the plan requires working with stakeholders to determine the objectives of the strategy and the values that the stakeholders want to uphold.

It is essential that the strategy is sufficiently broad and deep. Breadth refers to **incorporating the four main data types: health care, public health, social care and long-term care data**. Depth ensures that all data are included, and that they can be linked at the individual level to enable better care integration as well as more precision and scope in secondary uses. An important accompaniment to the digital strategy is a set of **roadmaps for each strategic objective**, particularly those that will be challenging to achieve, such as data interoperability.

To lead the development of the national strategy it is recommended that the Ministry:

- Builds trust and support for the strategy through **consultation with governmental and non-governmental stakeholders** on needs for information, analytics and information products
- Builds public trust through a **public information** campaign, public consultations and other avenues for **public input** into the strategy and provide a website to share information about the development process and its outcome.
- Considers developments in the Netherlands toward a **broader digital strategy** and ensure that the strategy for health data will be in alignment with them.
- Develops the **draft high-level IT architecture/infrastructure** for an integrated health information system that meets the information needs of key stakeholders including global standards for data exchange and semantic interoperability, privacy-by-design protections and interoperability in analytics, information and knowledge.
- Develops the **policy tools and financial incentives** to realise the strategy.

The ministry is recommended to further develop and **strengthen the national health data governance legislative framework** to support the national strategy. The framework should specify how to ensure uniform data and interoperability standards, enable the exchange, access to and use of data to serve the health-related public interest, protect privacy by design and align with EU regulations.

A national agency to implement and oversee the health information system

A single agency will be needed to **co-develop and implement the national strategy** with the Ministerie van Volksgezondheid, Welzijn en Sport (VWS) and oversee and maintain the resulting health information system. This could be done by 'strengthening' or combining expertise of existing organisations or creating a new agency.

The ministry is recommended to develop the **role and legal mandate** to launch the agency and to ensure that the governance of the agency provides a **formal involvement of key stakeholders** in the health information system.

1) It is recommended that the national agency take responsibility for four key activities that are essential to an integrated health information system:
2) Agreeing (or developing) and maintaining consistent **national standards** for terminology (semantics), data exchange (electronic messaging), analytics, data accessibility and sharing and harmonisation of data privacy and security policies and practices.
3) **Certification** including for vendors of IT solutions and digital tools for compliance with national standards; and verifying through quality checks and audits that health care providers and other information system actors have achieved interoperability standards and are exchanging useable (quality) data and are not blocking data flow.
4) Building and maintaining a **national public data platform** for public data exchange, acting as a hub through which the data flows. The platform should enable effective and secure processing of personal health data including data integration/linkage; foster adoption of a common health data model (CDM); manage the approval process for data integration and access requests involving data from multiple organisations; enable effective and secure mechanisms for access to personal health data for approved purposes, such as approved research; improving data quality, including

conducting data quality auditing; and reducing overlapping and duplicative administrative and data processing activities among key stakeholders within the health information system.

5) **Stakeholder engagement and public consultation** about the national strategy and its implementation; and **public transparency** about the national strategy and the development, exchange, uses and data privacy and security protections of health data.

References

Boyd M, Z. (2021), *Secondary Use of Health Data in Europe*, Open Data Institute, [4]
http://theodi.org/wp-content/uploads/2021/09/Secondary-use-of-Health-Data-In-Europe-ODI-Roche-Report-2021-5.pdf.

Dutch Tech Centre for Life Sciences (2021), *Health-RI*, https://www.dtls.nl/large-scale-research-infrastructures/health-ri/. [1]

EHDEN (2021), *European Health Data and Evidence Network*, https://www.ehden.eu/. [3]

ODISSEI (2021), *Open Data Infrastructure for Social Science and Economic Innovations*, [2]
https://odissei-data.nl/en/.

Notes

1   https://eenvandaag.avrotros.nl/item/gegevens-op-de-fax-of-een-dvd-bij-verplaatsing-van-coronapatienten-wordt-gemis-van-elektronisch-patientendossier-wel-heel-duidelijk/.

2 Privacy-by-design involves designing IT systems in a way that pro-actively anticipates and addresses risks to data privacy and security so they may be mitigated. In such approaches, the privacy of all individuals whose data is within the system is protected by default. The protection of individuals' privacy and data security is embedded within the architecture and functionality of the IT system. At the same time, the IT system supports all uses and re-uses of data that are in the public interest.

2 The structure and governance of the Dutch health information system in comparison with OECD countries

This chapter describes the relationship between the structure and organisation of the Dutch health system and the management, use and sharing of health data to improve health outcomes and achieve public policy objectives. The four fundamental laws that govern the four domains of the Dutch health system are discussed (public health, social care, curative care, and long-term care), which determine not only the health system's architecture but also how data are exchanged within it. The chapter then describes in more detail the concepts of health data infrastructure, data governance and an integrated health information system; the key components of an integrated health information system; and how it can help countries to advance policy objectives. Examples from across OECD countries illustrating the development of health data governance frameworks and interoperable electronic health record systems are presented to inform the review of the current situation in the Netherlands.

This chapter first outlines the key features of the Dutch health system in terms of its structure and organisation, and how these influence the generation, management and use of data. The scope includes the four laws that govern four domains of the Dutch health system: 1. public health, 2. social care, 3. curative care, and 4. long-term care. These laws lay the foundation for not only the overall structure of the health system but also how data flow between the various stakeholders and organisations within it. The result is a fragmented and heterogeneous health information landscape.

The second part of the chapter describes what is meant by a health data infrastructure and an integrated health information system, its key components, and how it can help countries advance policy objectives. Progress across OECD countries in the development of health data governance frameworks and in the development and governance of interoperable electronic health record systems are presented to inform the review of the current situation in the Netherlands.

The Dutch health system is fragmented by design

The Dutch health system (defined here as the overall approach to promote individual and population health through social, preventative and curative means) is a combination of managed competition where individuals, health care purchasers and providers determine price, quality and service based on supply and demand within policy and regulatory parameters set by the government (Van Driesden G, 2021[1]). The system is perhaps best viewed in terms of the laws that govern public health, social care, curative care and long-term care:

1. **Public Health Act:**
   a) Regulates public health interventions such as population-level screening and control of infectious disease
   b) Stipulates the remit of local governments in promoting public health and well-being.

2. **Social Support Act:**
   a) Stipulates that local governments are responsible for social support, informal care, and volunteer work
   b) Governs the provision of domestic help, day centres, support, and short-term stays at health facilities
   c) Requires sheltered accommodation for people with psychosocial problems.

3. **Health insurance Act:**
   a) Provides for basic entitlements to health care through the funding of basic health insurance
   b) Requires that individuals purchase basic health insurance
   c) Stipulates that health care providers may not exclude anyone from basic health insurance.

4. **Long-term Care Act:**
   a) Regulates health care for people who require 24-hour care and permanent supervision
   b) Provides that people who have received a special-needs assessment are entitled to care either at home or in a designated facility
   c) Requires that health care administrative offices procure sufficient care or provide personal budgets.

This arrangement creates the basic architecture for how Dutch health and social care data are collected, stored and managed (Figure 2.1). [1]

Figure 2.1. Four key types of health data in the Netherlands

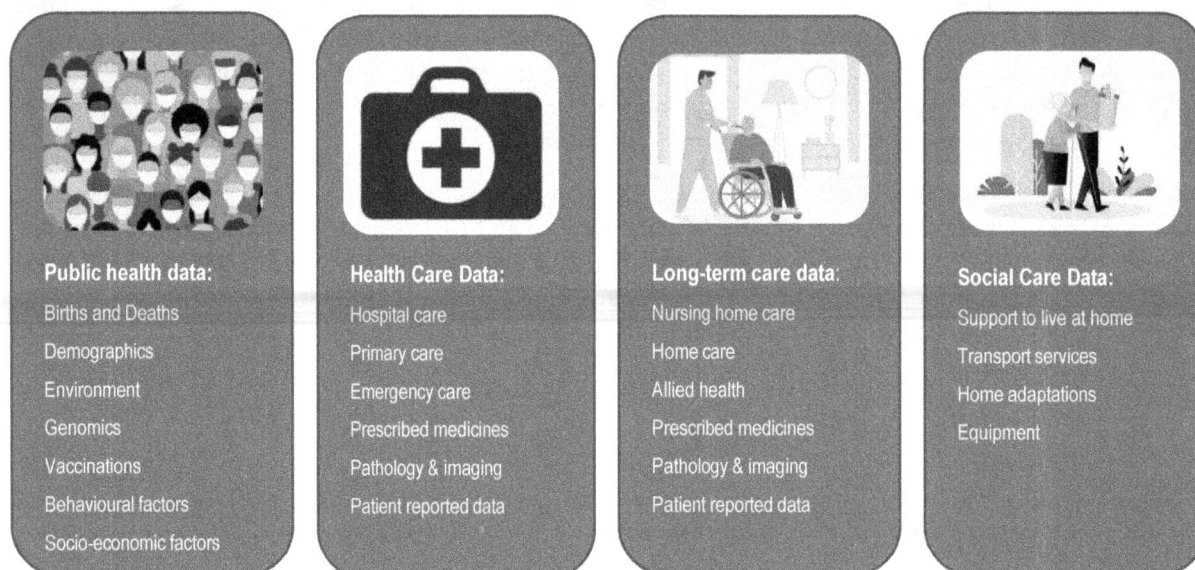

Public health data:	Health Care Data:	Long-term care data:	Social Care Data:
Births and Deaths	Hospital care	Nursing home care	Support to live at home
Demographics	Primary care	Home care	Transport services
Environment	Emergency care	Allied health	Home adaptations
Genomics	Prescribed medicines	Prescribed medicines	Equipment
Vaccinations	Pathology & imaging	Pathology & imaging	
Behavioural factors	Patient reported data	Patient reported data	
Socio-economic factors			

Image credits: © Shutterstock.com/Moab Republic, Shutterstock.com/Cube 29, Shutterstock.com/Millering, Shutterstock.com/Qualit Design.

In addition, the Dutch system works largely on a mixture of competition and market mechanisms, and it relies heavily on the private (not-for profit) sector. It has limited government involvement on a national level (health care) and substantive involvement on municipal level (social care). While it has performed very well in comparison to other OECD countries. It is highly fragmented across health settings and sectors – exemplified by the separate approaches toward managing and using public health data, health care data and social care data.

Fragmentation in health systems is certainly not unique. However, in contrast to other most countries where it is a result of either legacy factors or unintended policy consequences, it is a design feature in the Netherlands to ensure market mechanisms can function as intended. For example, the competition law explicitly prohibits exchange of information between providers in order to maintain the market mechanisms. However, an exchange of data can lead to actions that benefit public health, a role allocated to the government via the constitution law. This illustrates the need for some legal reform on data exchange for the benefit of public health.

Fragmentation and the consequent high number of data custodians – does not ipso facto impede nation-wide co-operation, co-ordination, and data standardisation, but it makes indispensable co-ordinated, national policies, legislations, incentives, and governance mechanisms to support and encourage actors toward the common goal of optimising the use of existing data.

Many institutional actors characterise the regulatory landscape of Dutch health and social care

Fragmentation characterises not only Dutch health system provision but also its regulation and governance. A high number of institutional actors and organisations have a stake in governance and regulation, data creation and processing, and data interoperability and exchange.

Governance and regulation

The key regulatory institutions, the **Nederlandse Zorgauthoriteit (NZa)**, the **Dutch Health Institute**, the **Inspection of health care and youth**, and the **Authority for Consumers and Markets**, all have part of the mandate in data governance and part access to the data. **Municipalities**, **health insurers** and **zorgkantoren** have siloed mandates for financing of health and social care.

The central government, meanwhile, is advised by different (independent) committees like the **Gezondheidsraad**, **Sociaal en Cultureel Planbureau**, **Wetenschappenlijke Raad voor het regeringsbeleid**, **Raad voor Volksgezondheid en samenleving** (curative care, long-term care, social care, and public health), **Zorginstituut Nederland** (curative care, long-term care), **Rijksinstituut voor Volksgezondheid en milieu** (RIVM), and the **GGD** (public health). The **Informatieberaad Zorg** (IB) is the (informal)advisory body in which parties come together to work towards safe exchange of information, however their focus is on curative care and primary uses of information.

The Dutch system also relies on input from confederations and representatives' organisations like the **Verbond van Nederlandse Ondernemingen en het Nederlands Christelijke Werkgeversverbond** (VNO-NCW), the **Federatie Medisch Specialisten**, Beroepsvereninging Verzorgenden Verpleegkundigen (V&VN), **Jeugdzorg Nederlan (JN)**, **Nederlandse Vereniging van Ziekenhuizen (NVZ)**, **the Nederlandse Federatie van Universitaire Medische Centra (NFU),** and the **Patiënten-federatie Nederland**.

Generating data, data processing and analytics capacity

Together, health and social care providers generate an immense amount of data but these data are most commonly kept within the organisation/sector. Some providers have realised the potential of integrating data with other providers and multiple initiatives to exchange data have started for example between collaborating hospital groups (**Santeon** group), regional health and social care provider alliances (**Beter Samen in Noord**), and municipalities and health insurers (gemeentezorgspiegel). However, not all providers have the capacity to do so, some are not able to access the data they generate for secondary purposes, due to a lack of human capital (skills) or financial resources for EHR data processing and analytics tools.

There is sharing of de-identified personal health data for secondary purposes, for example GP's sharing data with an academic network for primary care, is done within sector specific research organisations such as **Nivel** (health care), **Vilans** (long term care and social care), and **Trimbos** (mental health and addiction).

The Centraal Bureau voor de Statistiek (CBS) has a lot of experience in data processing, linkage and analytics. However, its mandate is limited in the health arena. The**)** in co-operation with CBS and the **Ministry of internal affairs** are trying to standardise data collection and use on a national level for all municipalities working with a diverse range of data from living conditions, education, economy, public health and social care. Noting that most individual municipalities, as most individual health and social care providers, do not have the capacity for data processing and analytics for secondary purposes.

Standard-setting for data content and exchange

Dutch claims data are well standardised and have clear custodianship. The **Nederlandse Zorgauthoriteit (NZa)** collects hospital activity data (DRG), **Vektis** collects reimbursement data, and the **Zorginstituut Nederland (ZiN)** collects data to enable risk equalisation among the many insurers in the Dutch health care market and public reporting on providers as part of the existing accountability mechanism.

Data on the quality of specialised care is most often managed through Quality Registries by professional networks and collected via private data custodians in specialised registries (e.g. **DICA, DHD, Dutch cancer registry**). Data generated by individual providers and health care professionals are less standardised as individual providers and provider organisations have different preferred tools (including indicators), EMR vendors (including some organisations with different content within the 'same' EMR system) and priorities in data standardisation. The **TWIIN** initiative co-ordinated by the Vereniging van Zorgaanbieders voor Zorgcommunicatie (**VZVZ**) and **RSO** Nederland has the overarching goal to lay the foundation of rules and infrastructure for these disparate entities to exchange data. The ambition is to create a data infrastructure with nationally co-ordinated authorisation and privacy design through: 1) exchange of medical images between health care providers, 2) exchanging laboratory results with pharmacies, and 3) exchange of data in perinatal health care. This initiative is not structurally funded but received start- up funding from **Zorgverzekeraars Nederland (ZN),** an umbrella organisation for Dutch health insurers.

The **Nederlands Normalisatie-Instituut (NEN)** is a non-for-profit private company and the Dutch collaborating partner with the European EN-norms and the international ISO-norms. Ministerie van Volksgezondheid, Welzijn en Sport has asked NEN to develop standards and certification schemes for electronic data exchange in health care together with the health care sector.

Nictiz is one of the important organisations developing standards for health data exchange in the Netherlands. Together with input from other parties that develop standards, like the **Zorginsituut Nederlands**, they have built up a library of standards on all five levels of interoperability 1) organisational, 2) process, 3) information, 4) application, and 5) IT-infrastructure.

There are initiatives to facilitate data exchange in health care. **Medmij** is a standard for the exchange of health care data between the care professional and the patient. Vendors of personal health environments can acquire the MedMij label to showcase safe and trustworthy data exchange practices. This initiative from the Informatieberaad Zorg and the Patiëntenfederatie Nederland is *voluntary* for vendors of personal health environments.

The **LSP**, co-ordinated by the **VZVZ**, is a platform in which patients/clients can authorise certain health care providers to share their data when needed. This platform started to facilitate access for health providers to patients' medication in *emergency situations*. It is an opt-in system and therefore does not cover the whole population. A proposal was recently heard in the senate that an opt-out system for health care data exchange would still maintain the right to choose and would be more fitting for the needs of patients.

Modern health systems (and societies) rely on integrated data and information

Twenty-first Century health systems will be built around information: the right information reaching the right person at the right time. This enables providing high-quality integrated care to all people in need, as well as better public health practice, health system management, and research and innovation. While health systems will continue to be structured, funded and organised differently, success – in terms of better care, public health, system management and research – will be characterised by a comprehensive, coherent, standardised and integrated approach to managing (electronic) health data.

A data infrastructure and information system

Any endeavour whose goal is social and economic advancement relies on infrastructure. Putting data to work successfully is no exception. **Data infrastructure** comprises data assets supported by people, processes and technology (Open Data Institute, n.d.[2]). It includes the bodies or institutions that create, maintain and manage the data as well as the institutions, policies and rules that guide their use. A data infrastructure can be seen as an ecosystem of technology, processes and actors/organisations needed for the collection, storage, maintenance, distribution and (re)use of data by the different end users. As an analogy, a rail infrastructure includes not only the tracks and trains but also the resources, people and equipment to maintain them, regulations and traffic control rules, as well as ticketing and other passenger services. A strong data infrastructure enhances the efficiency and productivity of using data.

It is necessary to distinguish between data and information. Data are raw figures and facts and, in and of themselves, may not be very valuable. Information, on the other hand, is meaning and insights that are obtained from the analysis of data. Thus, this report focusses on obtaining value from health data within the Netherlands by developing a system that yields information. A data infrastructure is the foundation. A **health information system** not only collects, manages, compiles standardises and exchanges data it also derives meaning and information from health data through analysis and review. It is a system because the focus is on data exchange and integration of information across different stakeholders. This requires supportive laws, policies, governance, hardware and software, expertise and analytical models as well as public communication channels, strategic planning, implementation guidelines, and audit and evaluation mechanisms.

An integrated health information system means that electronic data are FAIR (findable, accessible, interoperable, reusable), and can be exchanged and securely used by other actors and institutions that serve the public interest. The result is that data can flow, safely and securely, to where information can be extracted from them to create knowledge that advances human health and well-being.

Individual-level data are needed for both primary and secondary uses

An integrated health information system can help not only directly improve care quality, outcomes and patient empowerment by enabling patients and their health care providers to access important information, it would also raise the country's capacity to use these data for other important purposes including:

- Managing health system performance on national, regional and network level
- Public health monitoring and surveillance
- Opening new communications channels with patients to improve patient-centred care such as the active use of patient-reported metrics (PROMs and PREMs)
- Introduction of new digital services such as e-prescriptions or telehealth
- Better targeting of reimbursement for services to reward value
- Biomedical research and development
- Innovation such as big data analytics and artificial intelligence that will enhance knowledge-based decisions for patient care and health system governance.

Every data point should serve many uses, from informing a physician caring for a patient to helping patients manage their care, to health care quality monitoring indicators, value-based payments, real-world evaluation of the effectiveness of therapies and contributing to clinical decision support tools (artificial intelligence). Recent advances include that individuals' data are now used to inform decisions about their care and the care of others. The distinction between using data for primary purposes (direct patient care) and secondary purposes (e.g. research, public health monitoring) is therefore increasingly blurred.

For this reason, health data today cannot be easily categorised as personal or non-personal when the data pertain to individuals. A simple data processing step, such as removing personal identifying information like names, addresses, health insurance numbers and birth dates from a data set, does not yield anonymous data because it is increasingly easy to re-match the data to other datasets and re-identify individuals with some probability of success. More complex manipulations or aggregations of data to try to guarantee anonymity may destroy the quality, validity and usefulness of the data to produce valid information and research results.

Even the simple data processing step of removing personal identifying information must be carefully considered, as the linkage of datasets may require this information, for example to link hospital inpatients to mortality data to find out how many patients died in the weeks following a procedure. Mechanisms that allow re-identification for approved data uses, such as investing in pseudonymisation and secure storage of re-identification keys, are recommended by the OECD (see Annex B).

The key elements of an integrated system that enables primary and secondary uses of data are: approaching health data as a public good; implementing standardised data terminologies and formats (a single 'language'); a common data model and standardised analytics; and comprehensive data governance that uses a 'privacy-by-design' approach. These are outlined next, followed by a section on the interoperability of electronic medical records.

Approaching data as a public good

Countries making strides in putting their data to work have recognised that data are a valuable resource that should be used to generate public benefits. Significant public investment in health and health care are a key reason why health data are a public good – this includes public investment in health care provision, in health data development and in funding health research.

But there is also an economic argument for seeing data as a public good in the modern era of Big Data, high performance computing and modern analytical techniques including machine learning and artificial intelligence. Data represent immense value both because of the information they potentially contain and because they can be used and re-used ad infinitum. Their use by one actor does not preclude their use by others. More importantly, like other public goods such laws or language, data are instrumental in building social value through knowledge and information. Their exclusivity is not intrinsic, but is imposed by man-made laws, conventions, and institutions. In net terms, their commodification hampers human development.

Moreover, the social and economic value of data increase exponentially with their size. For example, a researcher looking for biomarkers that will uncover a precision therapy will find a single dataset comprising 10 million records is much more valuable than 100 separate datasets of 100 000 patients that cannot be linked or analysed as a whole (such as via the personal data train). In the private sector, forward-looking firms have realised that even a small slice of analytics on a huge data pool can generate far greater returns than hoarding much smaller puddles of data for proprietary use.

But to fulfil their potential in secondary uses as well as the primary objectives of improving patients' care, experience and outcomes, data held in various places by different custodians must be coded in formats and languages that enable them to be exchanged and linked.

Data must be standardised to common technical and semantic formats

The main reason why health data are not put to work is a lack interoperability. This happens when the information systems of data holders have been developed without the use of common standards which prevent data from being exchanged or when data are exchanged, make it very difficult for the data to be interpreted or integrated with other data. Without the ability to share and interpret data easily, every data exchange becomes a costly and time-consuming data integration project.

Data standards in health and health care include the methods, protocols, terminologies, and specifications for the collection, exchange, storage, and retrieval of health data from many different sources such as electronic medical records, insurance claims, laboratory test results, prescription medicine dispensing records, vaccination and public health records, population surveys and more (see Box 2.1).

Therefore, the most efficient solution to maximise the value of data held in silos is to agree on and adopt common standards for data terminology and exchange. Increasingly, such standards are becoming global, enabling multi-country collaboration in the development of IT systems and tools, cross-border access to clinical information for travellers who fall ill, as well as in undertaking multi-country medical and health research.

An intermediary solution exists to improve health data interoperability – mapping data from multiple organisations that use different data standards to a **Common Data Model (CDM)**. A CDM organises data into a standard structure that makes it possible for data and the meaning of data to be shared for analytical applications, allowing for efficient data pooling and data integration for health statistics and research. The

CDM is not, however, a practical solution for all situations where interoperability is needed such as the exchange of data among health care providers for direct patient care or the development of a patient portal.

It should be stressed that an integrated health information system does <u>not</u> require all data to be stored in a single location. It is quite possible to achieve the key objectives outlined earlier in this report without central storage or even aggregation. A unified and co-ordinated approach to national data governance can enable smooth information exchange and use for a range of purposes without compromising privacy, security and ownership of data. In fact, in some ways data protection can be enhanced under a federated data structure.

Further, ensuring that data can be exchanged across national borders into Europe and beyond can amplify the benefits of data analytics and research in, for example, the context of public health, rare diseases, pharmacovigilance, and precision medicine (see next section). An information system that follows international data standards facilitates within-country and cross-border health care delivery and business opportunities for the Netherland's research and technology sectors; and is better prepared to participate in and adapt to European regulations and initiatives.

Box 2.1. Data standards in health and health care

Data standards in health and health care describe the methods, protocols, terminologies, and specifications for the collection, exchange, storage, and retrieval of health data from many different sources including electronic medical records, insurance claims, laboratory test results, prescription medicine dispensing records, vaccination and public health records, population surveys and more.

Standardisation can be summarised as a three-step process. The first step is to specify and define **data elements.** Examples of data elements are a lab test result, a particular medicine, and a patient's name, age and allergies.

The next step is to associate **data types** with the data elements. Types include dates, time, counts, units (weights and measures) and codes that rely on formats and terminologies. For data to be exchanged and used for many purposes it is essential that the data types are universal and used consistently. A simple example is recording the time something occurred in a 24- or 12-hour format.

Many data elements are defined by terminologies and their associated codes. For example, SNOMED CT or SNOMED Clinical Terms is a systematically organised computer processable collection of medical terms providing codes, terms, synonyms and definitions used in clinical documentation and reporting. Standards for **syntax** are also required which specify how terms should be combined to be interpretable.

The third step is determining how to encode the data elements as an electronic message to exchange the data within the health information system. Message format standards include common encoding specifications, information models for defining relationships between data elements, and document architectures and clinical templates for structuring data as they are exchanged. A widely used standard for clinical record exchange is Health Level 7 (HL7).

Information models describe how elements and codes should be contextualised with additional information about data subjects. For example, the terminology and code for fever may be insufficient without also including information about the process for measuring the fever.

Document architectures are standards for classifying, capturing and revising clinical notes. Clinical templates impose constraints on an information model. For example, a message format for a laboratory test may have a clinical template that requires certain data elements to be included.

In addition to standards for data terminology and exchange, standards are also necessary for user interfaces, record linkage, and data privacy and security protections.

Standards should be accompanied by use cases.

A use case describes a particular instance of exchanging health data and includes the standardised data to be exchanged as well as the stakeholders involved and the legal framework supporting the data exchange.

Developing standards requires consideration of the data needs of all of the key stakeholders within the information system, including stakeholders requiring data for primary (direct care) and secondary (statistics and research) uses. Developing use cases alongside the development of data standards is a mechanism for ensuring that the standards will support the different uses of the data that will be needed.

Source: Institute of Medicine (2004[3]) "Health Care Data Standards", in *Patient Safety: Achieving a New Standard for Care*, https://doi.org/10.17226/; Schulz S., Stegwee R., Chronaki C. (2018[4]), "Standards in Healthcare Data", in *Fundamentals of Clinical Data Science*, https://doi.org/10.1007/978-3-319-99713-1_3.

The EU Health Data Space to help the region capitalise on the potential of health data

The considerable potential to advance health and welfare as well as providing commercial opportunities for European companies are the motivation to create an EU Health Data Space as part of the EU Digital Health Strategy (EC, 2021[5]). A new regulation is proposed to support Data Spaces in key economic sectors to create a single market for data, where data from public bodies, businesses and citizens can be used safely and fairly for the common good. An EU Health Data Space is proposed to "promote better exchange and access to different types of health data (electronic health records, genomics data, data from patient registries etc.), not only to support health care delivery (so-called primary use of data) but also for health research and health policy making purposes (so-called secondary use of data)" (EC, 2021a[6]).

Three pillars to support the Health Data Space are proposed:

1. Developing a health data governance framework for EU member states that provides guidance toward secure and privacy protective primary and secondary uses of health data that foster the accessibility and sharing of data. Such guidance would support greater harmonisation of the implementation of EU GDPR requirements in practice.

2. Data quality and interoperability including technical and semantic (terminology) interoperability between the different infrastructures and IT systems and ensuring health data in Europe are FAIR (Findable, Accessibly, Interoperable and Re-Usable).

3. Technical infrastructure that builds upon and scales up EU infrastructure, including the eHealth Digital Service Infrastructure, the European Reference Networks and the Genomics Project.

The technical and semantic interoperability standards for the Health Data Space are expected to include international standards for data exchange and terminology and favour exchange standards that support protection of health data privacy and security. For example, a 2021 policy report of the Standing Committee of European Doctors which represents medical associations across Europe, calls for the Health Data Spaces to adopt the HL7 FHIR standard for data exchange and the SNOMED CT clinical terminology standard (CPME, 2021[7]).

In alignment with the EU Health Data Space, the European Medicines Agency (EMA) is developing the DARWIN (Data Analysis and Real-World Interrogation Network) (EMA, 2021[8]). DARWIN will be a co-ordination centre to provide timely and reliable evidence on the use, safety and effectiveness of medicines for human use, including vaccines, from real world health care databases across the European Union (EU). The 2021 call for tender for DARWIN requires all bidders to implement a common data model (CDM).

New national bodies in France and Finland have characteristics and functions that are similar to the health data spaces envisaged by the EU. France introduced the Health Data Hub in 2019 and Finland launched FinData in 2020 to provide a unique entry point for secure and privacy-protective data linkage services and access to health microdata that are EU GDPR compliant (see next section for descriptions of FinData and the Health Data Hub).

Privacy by design and a national data governance framework are essential

A key component of a well-functioning health information system is data governance that avoids the over-use of consent to authorise data exchange, in favour of legal authorisation and requirements for an approach that protects privacy, ensures data security while enabling data to be exchanged and used for legitimate purposes. The OECD Council Recommendation on Health Data Governance sets out the elements for a national health data governance framework and fosters a 'privacy-by-design' approach that is consistent with emerging transnational requirements such as those set out in the EU General Data Protection Regulation (GDPR) (See Annex B).

Privacy-by-design involves designing IT systems in a way that pro-actively anticipates and addresses risks to data privacy and security so they may be mitigated. In such approaches, the privacy of all individuals whose data is within the system is protected by default. The protection of individuals' privacy and data security is embedded within the architecture and functionality of the IT system. At the same time, the IT system supports all uses and re-uses of data that are in the public interest (Cavoukian, 2006[9]).

Privacy-by-design is important because health data are often personal and sensitive, particularly health micro-data where there is a data record for each individual. The *EU Data Protection Regulation* (GDPR) [Regulation (EU) 2016/679 of the European Parliament and of the Council of 27 April 2016] places personal health data in a special category with the highest standards of protection.

The OECD Recommendation on Health Data Governance responds to the growing need for a consensus about the framework conditions within which health data can be appropriately governed to enable health data processing to take place both domestically and transnationally. Such health data governance frameworks require a whole of government approach; given that the public interests served span the domains of health, justice, industry, science, innovation and finance. The OECD Council Recommendation on Health Data Governance is compliant with the EU GDPR and encourages 'privacy-by-design'.

The OECD Recommendation on Health Data Governance was adopted by the OECD Council on 13 December 2016 and was welcomed by OECD Health Ministers at their meeting in Paris on 17 January 2017. The Recommendation provides policy guidance to:

- Encourage the availability and use of personal health information, to the extent that this enables significant improvements in health, health care quality and performance and, thereby, the development of healthy societies while, at the same time, continuing to promote and protect the fundamental values of privacy and individual liberties;

- Promote the use of personal health data for public policy objectives, while maintaining public trust and confidence that any risks to privacy and security are minimised and appropriately managed; and

- Support greater harmonisation among the health data governance frameworks of Adherents so that more countries can benefit from statistical and research uses of data in which there is a public interest, and so that more countries can participate in multi-country statistical and research projects, while protecting privacy and data security.

Governments adhering to the Recommendation will establish and implement a national health data governance framework to encourage the availability and use of personal health data to serve health-related public interest purposes while promoting the protection of privacy, personal health data and data security.

The Recommendation sets out 12 key elements of the development and implementation of national health data governance frameworks. The elements encourage greater cross-country harmonisation of data governance frameworks so that more countries can use health data for research, statistics and health care quality improvement.

The 2019/20 Survey of Health Data and Governance measured implementation of national health data governance frameworks and related regulations and policies. The 23 respondents to the 2019/20 survey were officials of national health ministries or national health data authorities.

A national health data governance framework can encourage the availability and use of personal health data to serve health-related public interest purposes while promoting the protection of privacy, personal health data and data security. Overall, 17 of 23 respondents reported that a national health data governance framework is established or is being established (Table 2.1).

Most respondents reported health data falling under a national health data privacy legislation; other data used in health studies falling under a national privacy legislation; and certain health datasets or health data programmes falling under other legislations governing ministries, data collections or registries. Some countries have legislations at different levels of government. Overall, 21 of 23 respondents reported that a national law or regulation exists that speaks to the protection of health information privacy and/or to the protection and use of electronic clinical records.

European Union (EU) member states implement the *European Union (EU) Data Protection Regulation (GDPR) [Regulation (EU) 2016/679 of the European Parliament and of the Council of 27 April 2016]*. The GDPR places personal health data in a special category with the highest standards of protection. Compliance requires that personal health data are very well organised and portable. For example, organisations must have data systems that allow them to fulfil individuals' rights to access their own personal data, to rectify or restrict their processing and to request data portability from one organisation to another; as well as to assure data are correctly categorised and demonstrate compliance with the regulation. In addition to national privacy laws compliant with the GDPR, most EU member states reported other national legislations with provisions specific to the protection of health data such as laws regarding patient rights, the collection and management of health information, the provision of medical care and health care organisations, electronic clinical record systems and health research.

Table 2.1. National health data governance elements

Respondent	A national health data governance framework is established or is being established	Public consultation has occurred or is planned about the elements of the national health data governance framework	National law or regulation exists that speaks to the protection of health information privacy and/or to the protection and use of electronic clinical records	A central authority for the approval of requests to process personal health data is established or planned
Australia	Yes	Yes	Yes	Yes
Austria	Yes	Yes	Yes	Yes
Belgium	No	No	Yes	Yes
Canada	Yes	Yes	No	No
Czech Republic	Yes	Yes	Yes	No
Denmark	Yes	No	Yes	Yes
Estonia	No	No	Yes	Yes
Finland	Yes	No	Yes	Yes
France	Yes	No[1]	Yes	Yes
Germany	Yes	No	Yes	No
Ireland	Yes	Yes	Yes	Yes
Israel	Yes	Yes	Yes	Yes
Japan	No	No	Yes	No
Korea	Yes	Yes	Yes	Yes
Latvia	Yes	Yes	Yes	Yes
Luxembourg	No	Yes	Yes	Yes
Netherlands	Yes	Yes	Yes	Yes
Norway	n.r.	n.r.	Yes	Yes
Singapore (non-Adherent)	No	Yes	Yes	No
Slovenia	Yes	Yes	Yes	Yes
Sweden	Yes	No	Yes	n.r.
United Kingdom (Scotland)	Yes	Yes	n.r.	Yes
United States	Yes	Yes	Yes	Yes
Total Yes	17	14	21	17

Note: Note: n.r.: not reported.

1. Mission of the Health Data Hub is to elaborate a citizens and patients charter in collaboration with patient associations.

Source: Oderkirk (2021[10]) "Survey results: National health data infrastructure and governance", https://doi.org/10.1787/55d24b5d-en.

Six respondents reported that their health data governance framework is set out in law (Austria, the Czech Republic, Denmark, Finland, France, Germany). In Austria, there are elements of data governance within legislation governing health telematics, documentation and research organisation. In the Czech Republic, the National Health Information System and its governance are defined in the *Act on Health Services*. Finland's health data governance framework is set out in legislation regarding digitisation and management of client and patient information as well as in regulations and guidelines of the health ministry (THL) (Box 2.2). Health data governance requirements, including GDPR requirements, are set out in federal and state laws in Germany.

Box 2.2. Finland – FinData

Findata is authorised by law to support the secondary uses of health and social data in Finland for projects that contribute to the public interest. Findata is the only authority that can issue permits for the secondary use of health and social data when the data is compiled from more than one data custodian. Findata provides for the secure linkage and research access to publicly funded datasets and registries including the data holdings of the Finnish Institute for Health and Welfare (THL), the Social Insurance Institution of Finland (Kela), the Population Register Centre, the Finnish Centre for Pensions and Statistics Finland. From 2021, Findata will expand to include data within the national EHR system (Kanta).

Findata is a centralised system issuing permits and a one-stop shop for the secondary use of health and social care data in Finland. It grants data use permits when data are requested from multiple registries or from the private sector; collects, links and prepares the data; provides the data in a secure IT-environment for data users; offers electronic tools for data permit applications; offers a help desk for data users; and works in collaboration with the controllers of the data.

Findata is not a permanent data repository, but a hub in which the data flows. It exists to streamline and secure the secondary use of health and social care data for four main purposes: 1) enabling effective and safe processing and access to data; 2) enhancing data protection and security; 3) eliminating overlapping administrative burden; and 4) improving data quality.

The *Act on the Secondary Use of Health and Social Data* (enacted in May 2019) gives Findata the authority to grant secondary use for research within Finland. It is noteworthy that this is made possible due to Finland's personal identification code that remains unchanged throughout an individual's life and is the key to linking personal information from various registries.

As a rule, the data are always disclosed to Findata's secure operating environment. However, the Act empowers Findata to make the data available in another environment as well, if it is necessary for the research purpose. These other environments will be audited for compliance with the regulation.

Source: Magazanik (forthcoming[11]), "Supporting Health Innovation With Fair Information Practice Principles: Key issues emerging from the OECD-Israel Workshop of 19-20 January 2021".

In France, principles of data governance are set out in an *Act on the Modernisation of the Health Care System* which unified the governance of administrative health data in the custody of three organisations and enabled dataset linkages and set out principles and procedures for data access. The 2019 *Act on the Organisation and Transformation of the Health System* broadened the definition of the national health data system to include additional datasets and their custodians and set out data sharing principles among these custodians. A Health Data Hub is defining the elements of shared data governance with stakeholders. The Health Data Hub (HDH) was launched in 2019 to support France in becoming a leader in Artificial Intelligence in health and to overcome barriers to the re-use of health data for research (Box 2.3).

Box 2.3. France: Health Data Hub

The HDH is a public interest group that was authorised by law and funded by the government to expand upon the existing national health data system (SNDS) to encompass all existing databases concerning publicly funded health activities (e.g. hospital electronic health records warehouses, cohorts, and registries). HDH was built on the infrastructure of the SNDS, the French administrative health care database that covers 99% of the population. The HDH catalogue unifies a collection of pseudonymised databases which the HDH is authorised to make available for research.

HDH's primary goal is to support research and innovation in health and health care by providing a unique entry point for secure and privacy-protective data linkage services and access to health microdata for research projects that contribute to the public interest, while respecting patient rights and ensuring transparency with civil society. The second goal was to design a state-of-the-art platform at the highest level of security, offering data storage, computing, risk mitigation and analysis capabilities. Finally, the third goal was to create a documented data catalogue built in a progressive manner to make priority data known to the scientific community.

The legal reform that launched the HDH aims to allow better visibility of common data assets for the entire ecosystem and to harmonise data access rules. Access to data is regulated and is carried out with respect for the rights of individuals. There is no obligation to process health data in France within the technological platform of the HDH and it is still possible to conduct research in other partnerships. HDH has so far launched 27 pilot projects, 9 of them COVID-19 related, after HDH received a specific mandate to accommodate COVID-19 related projects.

Permanent access to the HDH is granted to health authorities by decree of the French Ministry of Health. Other research requests for data are submitted to the "access team" that conducts a scientific and ethical assessment. If the request is found eligible, it is sent to the independent Scientific and Ethical Committee (CESREES). CESREES verifies that the purpose of the study is relevant and of public interest, that the data requested are in line with the study objective and that the proposed methodology is robust. If found positive, the project is submitted for authorisation of the French Data Protection Authority.

HDH consults with civil society by carrying out studies and consultations on the relationship that citizens have with health data and on their perceptions, needs and expectations. This knowledge is necessary to orient and adapt public communications, and to evaluate them and ensure they are clear. HDH also contributes to the implementation of a "health data culture" by providing educational tools to enable citizens to understand the data and to learn how to use them and how to carry out projects with them. (CNIL).

Source: Magazanik (forthcoming[11]), "Supporting Health Innovation With Fair Information Practice Principles: Key issues emerging from the OECD-Israel Workshop of 19-20 January 2021".

In the Netherlands, the Informatieberaad Zorg works on the development and sustainability of national health information and includes health care organisations and the Ministry of Health. The Council has four information system development goals: data to monitor the safety of prescription medicines; citizen access to their own medical data and the ability to link their own health and medical data; digitisation and exchange of data between health care professionals; and that data is recorded once and reused. A sub-group of the Council is the Community of Data Experts which advises the Council about the secondary use of health data for statistics, research and health and health care policy. Several laws include rules that make it mandatory to keep a medical record, to provide patients with digital access to their medical records and regarding system quality. A new framework law that passed the parliament in 2021 requires the electronic exchange of medical records among health care providers.

In Korea, the Ministry of Health established a health data governance framework in 2018 and set up a Healthcare Big Data Policy Deliberation Committee which is responsible for data development, use and dataset linkages. The COVID-19 pandemic has inspired an expansion of health data under a "Digital New Deal" which allows for the expansion and linkage of national health insurance data with other relevant data and for the accessibility of data for global research (Box 2.4). Latvia developed a Health System Performance Assessment Framework in 2019 (including health care quality, patient safety and efficiency indicators). Within this framework, principles and procedures for data provision, data linkage, health data protection, and access to data for research are set out.

Box 2.4. Korea: Digital New Deal

In Korea, the National Health Insurance (NHI) Database was established many years ago and organisations have been required to submit data to the NHI Program to obtain reimbursement. Korea already has real-time data at the national level across the continuum of health care services from insurance claims and these data are routinely linked for statistics and research.

The COVID-19 pandemic, however, has inspired an expansion of health data under a "Digital New Deal" that is being developed now. Under the New Deal, real-time insurance claims data can be linked with real-time clinical data. For example, Korea is developing the capability to monitor adverse events from the COVID-19 vaccination in real time. The Ministry of Health and Welfare and Health Insurance and Review Assessment Agency (HIRA) have been authorised to share COVID-19 data with the international community to find an effective response to COVID-19.

In order to further promote health data sharing for research, Korea has prepared legislation to establish a national data lake that will allow public bodies and private companies to have access to health data. Korea aims to link additional repositories to this national initiative. Under this new law (anticipated in 2021), Korea plans to maintain the data lake after the pandemic ends so it may continue to support international researchers' access to updated COVID-19 patient data.

De-identification techniques such as pseudonymisation are being used as a safeguard, and qualified organisations will perform data preparation. Engagement with the data lake is by application to qualified agencies.

Source: Magazanik (forthcoming[11]), "Supporting Health Innovation With Fair Information Practice Principles: Key issues emerging from the OECD-Israel Workshop of 19-20 January 2021".

The United States Department of Health and Human Services proposed in 2020 a new rule within the *21st Century Cures Act* to support seamless and secure access, exchange and use of electronic health records (Box 2.5). The rule aims to increase innovation and competition by giving patients and their health care providers secure access to health information; allowing more choice in care and treatment. A provision in the rule requires that patients can electronically access all their electronic health information (both structured and unstructured data) at no cost and deters blocking authorised access to and exchange of data. It calls on the health care industry to adopt standardised application programming interfaces (APIs) to allow individuals to securely and easily access structured electronic clinical data using smartphone applications.

The Department of Health and Human Services and the Office of the National Co-ordinator have also released a Trusted Exchange and Common Agreement (TEFCA) which sets out principles, terms and conditions for a common agreement to enable nationwide exchange of electronic health information across disparate health information networks. It aims to ensure that health information networks, health care providers, health plans, individuals and other stakeholders can have secure access to their electronic health information when and where it is needed.

Box 2.5. United States: New rule promoting access to data

In the United States, each state manages their own public health reporting programs, and these practices are regulated by state law. Each individual hospital system may have their own network – which can include thousands of payer systems. This fragmentation impedes patients' access to their complete records, as well as the availability of health data for research. To address this, the Department of Health and Human Services (HHS) proposed a new rule within the *21st Century Cures Act* to support the seamless and secure exchange and use of electronic health records. The rule asks the health care industry to utilise Application Programming Interfaces (APIs) and to adopt the HL7 Fast Healthcare Interoperability Resources (FHIR) standard for health data exchange. Further, a Trusted Exchange and Common Agreement (TEFCA) sets out principles, terms and conditions to enable the nationwide exchange of electronic health information across disparate health information networks.

Standardisation of the data sources is required for health data to be exchanged across all networks, not just the major networks like Medicare. The Office of the National Co-ordinator of Health IT (ONC) plans to introduce a the United States Core Data for Interoperability Standard, that will be the content and vocabulary baseline for health data, beginning 24 months after the publication of the final rule. This standard includes new data classes and data elements, such as provenance, clinical notes, paediatric vital signs, addresses, email addresses and phone numbers. These data pieces were not universally exchanged before – but are essential for patient matching and identifying risk factors. Leveraging this data allows better demographic information to be available to health care providers so that they can evaluate patients' risks and needs.

ONC has several pathways for public engagement and input into these data interoperability standards including a federal advisory committee made up of representatives from health care, health IT, and patient advocacy organisations. It publishes proposals for public comment and conducts targeted listening sessions with different groups. Finally, on the technical aspects, it works closely with the standards organisations which include public input and consensus- based balloting processes.

Generally, there isn't financial support to all stakeholders to invest in this, but there is some support for states to implement these capabilities in their networks. For health care providers, there was previously a programme that provided incentive payments for adoption of an electronic health record system, but there has not been new funding approved by Congress to continue support. However, there are requirements for hospital systems that are paid under the Medicare (National) programme to adopt and use technology that is certified to certain standards and functionalities. ONC has added these new requirements to the existing programme requirements. There is also a programme that requires the payers (the plans that administer Medicare and Medicaid) to build Application Programming Interfaces (APIs, as well to allow the data they hold to also be accessible. And finally, ONC requires technology developers, through a certification programme, to make this technology available to their customers.

Source: Magazanik (forthcoming[11]), "Supporting Health Innovation With Fair Information Practice Principles: Key issues emerging from the OECD-Israel Workshop of 19-20 January 2021".

In Australia, governmental responsibility for national health datasets is shared between Federal and State/Territorial jurisdictions. At each level of government, there are a range of agencies with responsibility for specific datasets and there is no overarching health data governance framework. However, all jurisdictions have signed the 2020-25 National Health Reform Agreement which includes an action to scale up a national approach to data governance arrangements, structures and processes, to facilitate clear and efficient mechanisms for sharing and developing data in a sustainable, purpose-based and safe way. There is an Australian data governance framework for electronic clinical data exchanged as part of the My Health Record System. A Data Availability and Transparency Bill was introduced in 2020 to implement a scheme to authorise and regulate access to Australian Government data (Box 2.6).

Box 2.6. Australia: Data Availability and Transparency Reform including the new Dataplace

Varying legislative requirements across the Commonwealth, States and Territories, particularly for privacy and permitted uses of data, have historically made data sharing more complex. Challenges to effective and efficient sharing and use of data are not limited to legislation. Technical, data availability and data quality challenges have affected the application of data from both new and well-established data assets to respond to the needs of the health system and the different needs Commonwealth, State and Territory data users.

The Office of the National Data Commissioner (ONDC) in Australia has been tasked with developing a new data sharing and release framework, and overseeing the integrity of data sharing and release activities of Australian Government agencies. The ONDC released its first guidance in 2019 – the Best Practice Guide to Applying Data Sharing Principles – which provides general guidance to assist agencies in adopting international best practices in data sharing.

The Australian Government introduced the *Data Availability and Transparency Bill 2020* (DAT Bill) into the Commonwealth Parliament in late 2020. Once passed, the Bill will establish a new scheme to safely share Australian Government data. To support the implementation of the new data sharing scheme, ONDC is establishing digital services (known as Dataplace) to manage: the accreditation process under the scheme; the submission of data requests to data custodians; and the negotiation, registration and management of data sharing agreements.

It is intended that Dataplace will eventually support the sharing of Australian Government data both under the new data sharing scheme and through other data sharing mechanisms.

The ONDC is also preparing to implement a Data Inventories Pilot Program to develop individual data inventories for Australian Government agencies using common standards and then to aggregate these inventories into an Australian Government Data Catalogue. The Pilot will initially cover about 20% of Australian Government entities. The Pilot will support greater transparency of government data holdings, facilitate data sharing and assist the Australian Government to respond quickly in emergencies.

An Intergovernmental Agreement on data sharing, agreed by the National Cabinet on 9 July 2021, committed the Commonwealth, State and Territory Governments to share public sector data (including health data) as a default position, where it can be done securely, safely, lawfully and ethically. The principles-based agreement recognises data as a shared national asset and aims to maximise the value of data to deliver outstanding policies and services for Australians. National effort will also be focussed on specific time-limited national priority data areas, under the Intergovernmental Agreement's National Data Sharing Work Program.

The 2020-25 Addendum to the National Health Reform Agreement has committed to a series of national action to enhance health data to enable long term health reform and harness data and analytics to drive meaningful improvements in the health system. This includes: establishing a national approach to govern the creation, access and sharing of data from all Australian Governments and progressing mechanisms and interoperable systems for secure and comprehensive integration of data across patient journeys.

Source: OECD Questionnaire on Health data and governance changes during the COVID-19 pandemic, 2021.

Ireland's Department of Health is currently working on a national health information strategy. In this strategy, Ireland is planning a National Health Observatory which would be authorised by law and include the development of a national health data governance framework.

In Israel, responsibilities for national health data governance are shared between the Ministry of Health and the Israel Innovation Authority. Israel's government has been working on designing a policy framework for secondary use of health data for research to enable collaborative data research initiatives. This framework is not yet finalised. As a result of the COVID-19 pandemic, the government has been accelerating work toward data sharing and access (Box 2.7).

Box 2.7. Israel: COVID-19 Data Lake

The Ministry of Health is working on an initiative to form a 'Data Lake' that will include Israel's digital health data from hospitals as well as HMO's and the Ministry of Health itself. On a national level, Israel has a rich and well computerised health data ecosystem consisting of 30 years of central public health care provided within HMOs serving 95% of patients. There is value in bringing all of this data together to accelerate COVID-19 related research. The 'Data Lake' policy framework consists of IRB certificate mechanisms, transparency, de-identification mechanisms, secure environment, user controls, opt-out mechanisms, and data use agreements.

The public interest in making the data available for research allows for an opt-out mechanism. Israel communicated with the public about the creation of the data lake via a text message to all persons. Strengthening the argument supporting the decision to offer an opt-out mechanism were previous decisions regarding the National Patient File (summary health record). The National Patient File requires all providers in Israel to use the same central system for data management, so that they can easily communicate with each other. There were discussions in the Ministry of Health to determine if this system should have an opt-in or opt-out structure. An opt-out structure was chosen because there was strong evidence that having all of the data available for patient care provides for more accurate findings and better health care services; and allows for more effective decisions to be made, which in turn allows costs to decrease and is in the public's best interest.

The COVID-19 Data Lake is only available for pure research with no collaboration with industry. There remain concerns that providing researchers access to the data lake may diminish public trust. In order to streamline the application process to the Data Lake, Israel is preparing one formal agreement for researchers that want to access the data, since this data is needed in a timely manner due to COVID-19. Further, Israel is considering new technologies for privacy enhancement that support researchers' ability to access complete records (raw data).

Source: Magazanik (forthcoming[11]), "Supporting Health Innovation With Fair Information Practice Principles: Key issues emerging from the OECD-Israel Workshop of 19-20 January 2021".

The Government of Canada, together with provinces and territories, is leading the development of a Pan-Canadian Health Data Strategy to improve Canada's collection, sharing and use of health data while protecting privacy. An Expert Advisory Group (EAG) was established in December 2020 to provide advice and guidance as work on the Pan-Canadian Health Data Strategy evolves.

Slovenia began developing a national health data governance framework in 2019. Luxembourg is planning a National Health Observatory which will be authorised by law and will support the development of a national health data governance framework. Belgium reported an intention to increase co-operation among several federal health administrations (Federal Public Service Health (FPS Health), RIZIV-INAMI, FAGG) regarding data policy.

The United Kingdom (Scotland) has an information governance framework for personal data, within which is a Public Benefit and Privacy Panel (PBPP) for health and social care data. The PBPP is a patient advocacy panel which scrutinises applications for access to NHS Scotland health data for secondary purposes with respect to the public benefit and privacy implications of proposed projects.

Legal or policy restrictions to public authorities extracting data from electronic health records

While many countries are extracting data from electronic clinical records to develop their key national datasets and for research (as will be discussed in the next section), 10 survey respondents in a 2019-20 survey on health data governance reported barriers to doing so.

In Luxembourg, data extraction from electronic clinical records for secondary uses is only lawful with the prior written consent of patients. Similarly, in Canada, electronic medical records in primary health care are in the custody and control of care providers who have no obligation and sometimes, depending on the jurisdiction, no legal authority to share data with public authorities, without express consent. As in Canada, the federal structure of Germany leads to different legal frameworks at the state level (state data protection laws, state hospital laws) that govern whether data may be extracted for secondary purposes. In Australia, data extraction is restricted by a number of legislative, privacy, secrecy and confidentiality requirements and medical records can be disclosed with consent, or in specified circumstances where authorised by law.

In France, extracting data from the electronic health record or DMP (dossier médical partagé) for the purposes of sharing and linking data is legally prohibited. France reports the legal prohibition came about because the national health insurance fund (CNAM) provides operational management of the linked health care administrative database and patients' associations sought a guarantee that clinical data within the DMP would not be accessible to the insurer. It is, however, legally possible to create a dataset of anonymised data from DMP records.

In Japan, there is no national electronic health record system within which data might be contributed by each medical institution. Further, medical institutions require patient consent for each research or statistical project where data would be extracted and shared from their electronic records.

In Korea, it is legally possible to extract data from electronic health records for secondary uses but the interpretation of the law is strict so doing so is difficult in practice. In Belgium there is no real policy about the extraction of data from electronic records for secondary uses. In Latvia, there is no experience yet with data extraction as the implementation of the national e-health system has only started recently. In Ireland, most health records remain paper-based in acute care hospitals.

Concerns were further echoed by respondents to the 2021 EHR survey. In 2021, 15 respondents reported that problems with the quality of data within electronic clinical record system created a barrier to developing national health datasets from this data source. The most common concern was with unstructured (free text) data within EHRs that need to be structured following common terminology standards to be readily useable for statistics and research. Thirteen respondents also reported legal or policy barriers to public authorities extracting data from within EHRs to develop national health datasets.

Perhaps the most difficult barrier is in Switzerland, where the law which authorises the creation of electronic clinical records did not foresee the use of data from within this information system for national statistics or research and, as a result there is a total ban on utilising this information resource for any purpose within the public interest other than directly caring for an individual patient. Similarly, in Korea, the law authorising the Information Exchange Program only authorised the exchange of EHR records for direct patient care and there is no legal basis for the secondary use of EHR data.

In Sweden, whether data can be extracted from EHRs for a statistical purpose is limited to the legal authorisation of the specific use. Statistics and research uses that have not been already foreseen and legally authorised are restricted. Similarly, Finland's law authorising the EHR system did not specify that health care quality monitoring could be undertaken with data from within the EHR system and are facing restrictions to this activity which is within the public interest. In Iceland, health data registries (datasets) are each authorised by a separate legislation. If a new registry (dataset) is needed, then it is necessary to pass a new legislation to authorise it. Similarly, Portugal reports a lack of legal authorisation to extract data for statistical purposes.

Japan and Turkey report concerns that the national data privacy law restricts their ability to extract data from within their EHR systems to build national datasets that are within the public interest. Canada reports the challenge of having different data protection laws within its 13 provinces and territories.

EU Members are also reporting challenges implementing the EU General Data Protection Regulation (GDPR). Italy reports that the GDPR provisions are complex and require the involvement of the data protection authority to develop effective solutions that support extraction of data from EHRs for statistical purposes. Similarly, Slovenia reports that the national legislation is very sophisticated and restrictive which limits their ability to extract data for statistical purposes.

In the Netherlands, problems have arisen following the introduction of the EU GDPR. Dutch health datasets are in the custody of various public sector organisations (such as the Dutch Hospital Data institute, and the Perined (child birth data) institute). Among the custodians of health data, there are different interpretations of the EU GDPR and some have determined that past data exchange arrangements are no longer legally permitted. To clarify that data exchange is lawful, some organisations and institutes are asking government for legislation authorising the exchange of electronic clinical data (see Chapter 3 for further discussion).

EMR interoperability is critical with success characterised by co-ordination and leadership at the national level

Clinical data are a key component of any health information system looking to improve care quality as well as enabling research and innovation. This section outlines the current situation in OECD countries regarding the exchange and interoperability of electronic health records data, and the key elements of successful integration.

Exchange of clinical data at the national level

Most OECD countries, 21 of 27 countries surveyed in 2021, are exchanging electronic clinical records among physicians, medical specialists and hospitals for the direct care of patients. Sixteen countries report one country-wide EHR system is in place. Thirteen countries reported that a nationally standardised patient summary is exchanged among health care providers at a national level, and a broader array of patient data are exchanged among health care providers at the sub-national (state, regional) level. In three countries, Belgium, Canada and the Czech Republic, patient data is exchanged among health care providers only at the sub-national (regional, state) level.

A single authority to oversee EHR development and interoperability

In 2021, the OECD surveyed countries regarding the readiness of their electronic health record systems to contribute to national information and research. Twenty-three of 27 countries reported a national organisation with primary responsibility for national EHR infrastructure development. Twenty countries reported that their national organisation is responsible for setting national standards for both clinical terminology within EHRs and standards for data exchange (electronic messaging).

Table 2.2. National organisation responsible for EHR system and its role

Country	National organisation with primary responsibility for national EHR infrastructure development	Name of the organisation	National organisation sets standards for clinical terminology in Electronic Health Records	National organisation sets standards for electronic messaging	Other major responsibilities of this national organisation
Australia	Yes	Australian Digital Health Agency (ADHA)	Yes	No[5]	Coordinates and reviews Australia's National Digital Health Strategy.
Belgium	Yes	eHealth Platform and FPS Health	Yes	Yes	National eHealth services
Canada	Yes[1]	Canada Health Infoway	Yes	Yes	Accelerates the development, adoption and effective use of digital health solutions. Independent, not-for-profit organisation established in 2001 and funded by the federal government.
Costa Rica	No		n.a	n.a	
Czech Republic	Yes	Ministry of Health, Department of Informatics and Electronic Healthcare (ITEZ)	Yes[6]	Yes[6]	Focuses on the e-health strategy and maintenance of national information standards. Implementation of the infrastructure is provided by UZIS.
Denmark	Yes	Danish Health Data Authority	Yes	Yes	National registries, secondary use of data, statistics in health and reimbursement schemes
Estonia	Yes	Centre of Health and Welfare Information Systems	Yes	Yes	Organises and co-ordinates the administration of ICT development and management of strategies, development plans and budgets. Role includes strategic planning of information systems and e-services; advise to government; responsibility for information systems and databases; improvement of the interoperability and exchange of information of e-solutions; integrated management of the IT architecture; development and management of cross-border data exchange services; services, software and information systems procurement; implementation of best practices for the protection of personal data; implementation of the information security policy; monitors the use and security of information systems and compliance information security regulations; inspections, as necessary of information systems, data integrity and security. Responsible for ICT under the MoH including infrastructure, data communications, data security, backup, systems administration; software support for ICT, ICT governance and development, systems integration, maintenance and computer support, and user support services. data transmission formats, data control rules and data transmission systems related to information systems; development and management of classifications; management of technical data quality related to information systems; creates and manages a data warehouse which enables to fulfill the tasks assigned to the processor authorised by legislation
Finland	Yes	Social Insurance Institution (Kela)	Yes	Yes	National rules and mandatory requirements for systems
Germany	Yes	Gematik GmbH	n.r.	n.r.	
Hungary	Yes	Ministry of Health and Director General	n.r.	n.r.	General country-wide responsibility for health care systems

Country	National organisation with primary responsibility for national EHR infrastructure development	Name of the organisation	National organisation sets standards for clinical terminology in Electronic Health Records	National organisation sets standards for electronic messaging	Other major responsibilities of this national organisation
		of National Hospitals (OKFO)			
Iceland	Yes	Directorate of Health, National Centre for eHealth Unit	Yes	Yes	Development and implementation of national digital solutions in health care, including the integrated electronic health record and the national patient portal, eHealth strategies, clinical terminology standards and the Icelandic HealthNet.
Israel	No[2]	Ministry of Health	Yes	Yes	
Italy	Yes	Ministry of Economy, SOGEI (in-house system integrator)	Yes	Yes	Sets strategic objectives, evaluates the ongoing activities and results, and defines the functional and technical specifications for EHR documents.
Japan	Yes	Health Insurance Claims Review and Reimbursement Services and All-Japan Federation of National Health Insurance Organisations	Yes	Yes	Payments of medical fees, system implementation supports, etc.
Korea	Yes	Korean Health Information Service (KHIS)	Yes	Yes	Department responsible for developing EHR infrastructure including standardisation, personal health records (PHR), health information data exchange, and certification (criteria development, business, education). A separate department is established for EHR data utilisation.
Lithuania	Yes	Ministry of Health and State Enterprise Centre of Registers	Yes	Yes	Formulates state policy, organises, co-ordinates and controls its implementation, including digitisation of health care sector and is the controller of the State Electronic Health Services and Co-operation Infrastructure Information System (ESPBI IS)
Luxembourg	Yes	Agence eSanté	Yes	Yes	Set up and operate a national electronic platform for the exchange and sharing of health date; promote interoperability and security in health information systems; establish and maintain roadmap for health information systems; assist regulators and authorities on strategic choices related to health information systems; and disseminate information on operational procedures and security measures.
Mexico	n.r.		n.r.	n.r.	
Netherlands	Yes	n.r.	Yes	Yes	National Health Information Council (Informatieberaad zorg). In that council both health care organisations and the Ministry of Health work on the sustainability of the information framework in health care. Four goals are: 1) safety of prescribing, 2) citizens can see their own medical data and link these to their own health data, 3) digital and standardised transfer of data between health professionals, 4) data is recorded once and then reused.
Norway	Yes	Norsk Helsenett	No[7]	No[7]	Develop, manage and operate national e-health solutions, core journal and e-prescription, as well as basic data in various registers and provide the national infrastructure for electronic communication in the health sector.

Country	National organisation with primary responsibility for national EHR infrastructure development	Name of the organisation	National organisation sets standards for clinical terminology in Electronic Health Records	National organisation sets standards for electronic messaging	Other major responsibilities of this national organisation
Portugal	Yes	SPMS (Shared Services for the Ministry of Health, EPE)	Yes	Yes	Public enterprise created in 2010 under the guardianship of the Ministries of Health and Finance. Provides shared services to health organisations: ICT, purchasing and logistics, financial services and human resources and centralises the procurement of goods and services within the NHS. SPMS is a corporate legal entity with administrative and financial autonomy and its own assets. SPMS is a Competence Centre with the main responsibility of implementation and operation of Health Information Systems to be used in the Portuguese Health System and it is the national authority for eHealth cross border co-operation. SPMS promotes the definition and use of standards, methodologies and requirements that guarantee interoperability and interconnection of health information systems with each other and with cross-sectional information systems of the Public Administration. It works with other EU countries to share knowledge and to align and adopt common standards (e. g. HL7 and IHE).
Russian Federation	Yes	Ministry of Health and Ministry of Digital Development, Communications and Mass Media	Yes	Yes	
Slovenia	Yes	National Institute of Public Health (NIJZ)	Yes	Yes	Public health authority
Sweden	Yes and No[3]	Multiple agencies involved at national and regional levels	Yes	Yes	Coordination of eHealth initiatives among regional health authorities
Switzerland	Yes	eHealth Suisse	Yes	Yes	Creation and update of the conceptual basis for the EHR certification process; creation and update of the requirements of the central components / services necessary for a running EHR (metadata index, community portal index services, HP index service and others /run by the Federal Office of Information Technology, Systems and Telecommunication FOITT; and EHR information and co-ordination
Turkey	Yes	Ministry of Health	Yes	Yes	
United States	No[4]		n.a.	n.a.	

Notes: n.r. Not Reported // n.a. Not Applicable // d.k. Unknown.

1. Canada Health was in a lead role for the development and implementation but it is managed by each jurisdiction.

2. EHR are regulated by the Ministry of Health.

3. Some aspects are co-ordinated between a few authorities.

4. US Department of Health and Human Services adopts national standards and regulates the certification of EHR products. Governance of the exchange infrastructure is currently being defined.

5. ADHA specifies which messaging standards are required to allow other clinical systems and mobile applications to connect with the My Health Record System.

6. MoH recommends standards. Legislation is in preparation to create a legal mandate to enforce e-Health related standards.

7. Norwegian Directorate for e-health is responsible to set standards for clinical terminology and data exchange.

Source: OECD 2021 Survey of Electronic Health Record System Development, Use and Governance.

Fourteen countries reported in 2021 that the national organisation responsible for EHR infrastructure development had a multidisciplinary governing body with representation from various stakeholder groups. Multi-disciplinary governance supports the development of standards that meet the needs of different stakeholders in the health information system.

Table 2.3. National organisation has a multidisciplinary governing body

Country	Governing body of the national organisation is multi-disciplinary with representation from various stakeholder groups	Stakeholder groups represented within the governing body of the national organisation
Australia	Yes	Governed by a Board and a person is eligible for appointment as a Board member only if the Health Minister is satisfied that the person has skills, experience or knowledge in at least one of the following fields: medical practice; health informatics, health technology standards and information management in large scale health settings; health care delivery; delivery of private health services; consumer health advocacy; designing, developing and delivering innovative uses of technology; developing, implementing and managing national digital health policies, strategies and services; developing, implementing and operating clinically safe work practices, methods and patient safety solutions in relation to digital health services; financial management; providing legal services and advice; managing and delivering digital health systems in State and Territory health facilities; and leadership and management in the delivery of traditional and digital health services that are managed, operated or provided by a State or Territory Government.
Belgium	Yes	Involves all health stakeholders: health care providers and organisations, patients, mutual funds, public institutions, Communities and Regions, etc.
Canada	No	Membership of Infoway is Deputy Ministers of Health for the Federal, Provincial and Territorial Governments. Infoway is responsible for engaging a wide variety of stakeholders (clinicians, patients, governments, vendors, academia, etc.)
Costa Rica	n.a	
Czech Republic	n.r.	
Denmark	No	
Estonia	No	
Finland	Yes	THL and Kela have, to some extent, a multi-disciplinary employee base and have multi-disciplinary stakeholder groups and steering mechanisms.
Germany	Yes	Shareholders are the Federal Ministry of Health (BMG), the Federal Medical Association (BÄK), the Bundeszahnärztekammer (BZÄK), the German Association of Pharmacists (DAV), the German Hospital Association (DKG), the Central Association of Statutory Health Insurance Institutions (GKV-SV), the Federal Association of Statutory Health Insurance Physicians (KBV), the Association of Statutory Dentists (KZBV) and the Private Health Insurance Association (PKV).
Hungary	No	
Iceland	Yes	Health professionals and relevant stakeholder groups are contacted to form working groups to work on different eHealth projects. Moreover, health professional surveys and citizen surveys are conducted on a regular basis.
Israel	Yes	
Italy	Yes	Representatives of the institutions (different Ministries and Regions) and stakeholders: doctors, nurses and apothecaries associations, and municipalities associations.
Japan	No	
Korea	No	
Lithuania	No	
Luxembourg	Yes	Agence eSanté GIE is established in the form of an Economic Interest Grouping which counts as members the major health care related stakeholders, namely: Luxembourg State represented by the Ministry of Health and the Ministry of Social Security; National Health Fund (Caisse Nationale de Santé); Social Security Office (Centre Commun de la Sécurité Sociale); Association of Doctors and Dentists (Association des Médecins et Médecins-Dentistes); Luxembourg Hospital Federation (Fédération des Hôpitaux Luxembourgeois); Confederation of long term and home care providers (Confédération des organismes prestataires d'aides et de soins; Luxembourg federation of laboratories (Fédération Luxembourgeoise des Laboratoires d'Analyses Médicales); the association of Pharmacists (Syndicat des

Country	Governing body of the national organisation is multi-disciplinary with representation from various stakeholder groups	Stakeholder groups represented within the governing body of the national organisation
		Pharmaciens Luxembourgeois); Association for the Defence of Patients' Interests (Patientevertriedung).
Mexico	n.r.	
Netherlands	Yes	
Norway	Yes	
Portugal	Yes	It includes several workgroups including stakeholders.
Russian Federation	No	
Slovenia	No	It is a public institution, appointed by the Ministry of Heatlh. Other stakeholders are involved indirectly.
Sweden	Yes	Coordination of eHealth initiatives among regional health authorities
Switzerland	Yes	All relevant stakeholders groups included such as political authorities (federal level and cantons), physicians, other HPs associations, hospitals, insurances and so on.
Turkey	Yes	Personnel of the health care system that is developed and managed by Ministry of Health.
United States	n.a.	

Source: OECD 2021 Survey of Electronic Health Record System Development, Use and Governance.

Convergence towards specific standards is occurring

Global consensus regarding terminology standards for key clinical terms has not been reached yet. There are, however, a few international terminology standards that are used by a significant share of countries.

In 2021, 18 respondents reported using the International Statistical Classification of Diseases and Related Health Problems, 10th Revision (**ICD-10**) for diagnostic terms; 16 respondents reported the Anatomical Therapeutic Chemical (**ATC**) Classification System for medication terms; 13 respondents reported the Logical Observation Identifiers Names and Codes (**LOINC**) for laboratory test terms; and 10 respondents reported **DICOM** standards for medical image terms. These results for 2021 are a small improvement from 2016, as the number of respondents adopting the ICD-10 diagnostic terms and ATC medication terms has grown by a few countries.

Twelve respondents reported adopting the Systematised Nomenclature of Medicine-Clinical Terms (**SNOMED CT**) for at least one key term within their EHR. SNOMED CT is a comprehensive set of terminology standards covering key terms within EHR records. The cost of deployment; however, is a barrier to widespread adoption and the number of respondents is unchanged from 2016.

However, there remain key terms within clinical records where there is no consensus among countries about which international standard could apply. These include surgical procedures, vital signs, healthy behaviours, socio-economic status, clinically relevant cultural and psychosocial characteristics, and patient reported outcomes and experiences. Further, there are often local standards that have been adopted or, in some cases, these elements are not coded to a terminology standard but recorded as free text.

The legacy of fragmented deployment of EHRs has resulted in 11 respondents reporting clinical terminology standards are inconsistent among different networks or regions within their country. While this remains a significant problem, it has improved from 2016 when 20 respondents reported this issue.

Twenty-one respondents in 2021 reported implementing policies or projects to improve the interoperability of data within electronic health record systems (EHRs). Seventeen respondents are adopting the HL7 Fast

Healthcare Interoperability (Resource) standard and a further two respondents are considering adoption. The **HL7 FHIR** standard supports web-based applications in health care as they exist for other sectors such as for e-commerce, banking, and travel booking; and utilises commonly used web development tools which allow for a larger pool of developers and faster development.

Twelve respondents are also adopting **SMART** on FHIR standards (or similar) and a further 4 respondents are considering adopting SMART on FHIR. Substitutable Medical Applications and Reusable Technologies (SMART) is a standard used on top of FHIR to develop web-browser and mobile/smartphone apps that can be connected to/interact with any EHR system. For example, an app to assist patients with managing their medications or an app for secure communication with a health care provider.

Fourteen respondents reported developing public application programming interfaces (**APIs**) and an additional respondent is considering adopting this standard. Application programming interfaces (APIs) allow data sharing among different EHR software and Health Information Technologies, overcoming blockages to data interoperability.

Table 2.4. Interoperability standards

Respondent	Implementing policies or projects to improve EHR interoperability	Developing public application programming interfaces (APIs)	Adopting HL7 Fast Healthcare Interoperability Resource (FHIR) standard	Adopting SMART on FHIR standards
Australia	Yes	Yes	Yes	Yes
Belgium	Yes	Yes	Yes	Yes
Canada	Yes	Yes	Yes	No
Costa Rica	No	No	No	No
Czech Republic	Yes	n.r.	Yes	Yes
Denmark	Yes	Yes	Yes	No
Estonia	Yes	No	Yes	Yes
Finland	Yes	Yes[1]	Yes	Yes
Germany	n.r.	n.r.	n.r.	n.r.
Hungary	Yes	Yes	No	No
Iceland	Yes	Yes	Yes	No[2]
Israel	Yes	No	Yes	No[2]
Italy	Yes	No	Yes	No
Japan	Yes	No	No[2]	No[2]
Korea	Yes	Yes	Yes	Yes
Lithuania	Yes	No	Yes	Yes
Luxembourg	Yes	Yes	Yes	No
Mexico	n.r.	n.r.	n.r.	n.r.
Netherlands	Yes	Yes	Yes	Yes
Norway	Yes	Yes	Yes	Yes
Portugal	No	Yes	No	n.r.
Russian Federation	n.r.	n.r.	Yes	Yes
Slovenia	Yes	n.r.	No	n.r.
Sweden	Yes	Yes	Yes	Yes
Switzerland	Yes	No[2]	No[2]	No[2]
Turkey	No	Yes	No	Yes
United States	Yes	No	No	No
Total Yes	21	14	17	12

Notes: n.r. Not Reported // n.a. Not Applicable // d.k. Unknown.
1. May not be open (public).
2. In consideration for adoption.
Source: OECD 2021 Survey of Electronic Health Record System Development, Use and Governance.

Global collaboration towards common standards

Encouragingly, respondents reported participation in global collaborative work toward agreed international standards for clinical terminology and data exchange (electronic messaging). In 2021, 15 respondents reported participating in the Integrating the Healthcare Enterprise International collaboration and 10 respondents reported participating in the Global Digital Health Partnership.

There is extensive work underway within the European Union (EU) toward improving the accessibility, sharing and use of health data that, if successful, would have an influence on the evolution of global collaboration in the sharing, use and protection of health data. A key EU project is the eHealth Digital Service Infrastructure (eHDSI) for cross-border health data exchange under the Connecting Europe Facility (CEF) that is supporting EHR data exchange at the country level and the provision of core services at the EU level.

Another key project is the Joint Action Towards the European Health Data Space (TEHDAS). TEHDAS is developing European principles for the secondary use of health data, building upon successful development of health data hubs in a few countries, such as France and Finland, and aiming to develop health data governance and rules for cross-border data exchange, improve data quality and provide strong technical infrastructure and interoperability (EC, 2021[5]). The European Health Data Space has the potential to act as a powerful federator between national data hubs, promoting interoperability standards, best practices for data sharing across the European Union and setting a coherent governance framework.

Table 2.5. Global collaborations for exchange and terminology standards

Respondents	IHE (Integrating the Healthcare Enterprise) International	Global Digital Health Partnership	EU projects to facilitate sharing and utilising EHR data across EU member states
Australia	No	Yes	No
Austria	Yes	Yes	Yes
Belgium	Yes	No	Yes
Canada	n.r.	Yes	No
Costa Rica	No	No	No
Czech Republic	Yes	n.r.	Yes
Denmark	Yes	No	Yes
Estonia	Yes	Yes	Yes
Finland	Yes	No	Yes
Germany	n.r.	n.r.	Yes
Hungary	No	No	Yes
Iceland	No	No	Yes
Israel	No	No	No
Italy	No	No	Yes
Japan	Yes	Yes	No
Korea	No	Yes	No
Lithuania	Yes	No	Yes
Luxembourg	Yes	No	Yes
Mexico	n.r.	n.r.	n.r.
Netherlands	Yes	Yes	Yes
Norway	n.r.	n.r.	Yes
Portugal	Yes	Yes	Yes
Russian Federation	n.r.	n.r.	n.r.
Slovenia	No	No	Yes
Sweden	Yes	No	Yes

Respondents	IHE (Integrating the Healthcare Enterprise) International	Global Digital Health Partnership	EU projects to facilitate sharing and utilising EHR data across EU member states
Switzerland	Yes	Yes	No
Turkey	Yes	No	Yes
United States	Yes	Yes	No
Total Yes	15	10	18

Notes: n.r. Not Reported // n.a. Not Applicable // d.k. Unknown.
Source: OECD 2021 Survey of Electronic Health Record System Development, Use and Governance.

The 2021 survey also asked respondents about the coding of health data to CDMs which facilitate within country statistical and research projects. In 2021, five respondents reported coding data within their EHR systems to a CDM. When the common data model is international in scope, such as the OMOP (Observational Medical Outcomes Partnership) CDM, such coding efforts support internationally comparable data for a wide array of research and statistical uses. There were some applications of the OMOP CDM reported by Australia and Israel in 2021. The Health Insurance Review and Assessment Agency (HIRA) in Korea coded linked health data to the OMOP CDM, including HIRA's national insurance claims data, for the purposes of encouraging secure access to timely data for global COVID-19 research as part of the OHDSI project. France is coding data within the Health Data Hub to the OMOP CDM as part of the EU EHDEN project which is affiliated with OHDSI.

Approaches to data storage and management vary

Surprisingly, given the mounting volume of data created, only 8 of 26 respondents in 2021 reported that EHR data are stored or processed using Cloud Computing services (Australia, Israel, Japan, Korea, Luxembourg, the Netherlands, Portugal and the United States). The majority of respondents are still managing EHR data on dedicated servers.

Essential to data security, integration and patient safety are unique identifiers. In 2021, 24 of 27 countries reported that they have a unique national number that identifies patients to build and electronic health record. Further, 23 countries reported having a unique national number that identifies health care providers or other authorised persons who are entering data into an electronic health record.

Fourteen respondents reported that clinical data are encrypted when they are exchanged to protect privacy and data security. Nine respondents reported that clinical data are exchanged using a dedicated, secure network. Security measures for these networks included a digital signature for ID (Denmark), digital signature with smartcard (Luxembourg, the Netherlands), multi-factor authentication (Canada, Italy, the Netherlands, Switzerland), digital certificates for ID verification (Japan, Lithuania), virtual safeboxes for data exchange (Israel), channel encryption (Italy), and IP security and Internet key exchange (Japan). A few respondents also noted data de-identification and pseudonymisation (Italy) and even data anonymisation (Costa Rica).

Respondents reported methods they are using to secure EHR data from unauthorised access, hacking and malware. These include virus scanning, firewalls, controlled access, access logs, audit logs, automated log-out, timely software updates, network separation, auditing hardware and databases, physical security for networked hardware, staff training in data security including how to identify phishing schemes, malware and other malicious programs, penetration tests (ethical hacking), vulnerability scanning, national authorities supervising cybersecurity among data processors, and business continuity and disaster recovery planning.

Legislation requiring adoption of Electronic Health Record Systems that conform to national standards

In the 2021 survey, 17 respondents reported that there are laws or regulations requiring health care providers to meet standards for national electronic health record interoperability. Sixteen respondents reported that laws or regulations require electronic messaging standards and 16 also respondents reported that laws or regulations require terminology standards.

Table 2.6. Laws or regulations require standards for EHR interoperability

Respondent	Laws or regulations require clinical terminology standards	Laws or regulations require electronic messaging standards	Laws or regulations require health care providers meet standards for national EHR interoperability
Australia	No	No	No
Austria	Yes	Yes	Yes
Belgium	No	No	No
Canada	n.r.	n.r.	n.r.
Costa Rica	Yes	Yes	Yes
Czech Republic	n.r.	n.r.	n.r.
Denmark	No	No	Yes
Estonia	Yes	Yes	Yes
Finland	Yes	Yes	Yes
Germany	n.r.	n.r.	n.r.
Hungary	Yes	Yes	Yes
Iceland	Yes	Yes[1]	Yes
Israel	Yes[2]	No	No
Italy	Yes	Yes	Yes
Japan	Yes	Yes	Yes
Korea	Yes	Yes	Yes
Lithuania	Yes	Yes	Yes
Luxembourg	No	Yes	Yes
Mexico	n.r.	n.r.	n.r.
Netherlands	Yes	No	No
Norway	n.r.	n.r.	Yes
Portugal	No	Yes	No
Russian Federation	Yes	Yes	Yes
Slovenia	Yes	Yes	Yes
Sweden	n.r.	n.r.	n.r.
Switzerland	Yes	Yes	Yes
Turkey	Yes	Yes	Yes
United States	n.a.	n.a.	n.a.
Total Yes	16	16	17

Notes: n.r. Not Reported // n.a. Not Applicable // d.k. Unknown.
1. Law recommends the use of EHRs.
2. For diagnosis.
Source: OECD 2021 Survey of Electronic Health Record System Development, Use and Governance.

Certification of electronic health record system software vendors

In the 2021 EHR survey, 16 respondents reported that they have a certification process for the vendors of electronic health record system software that requires vendors to conform to particular health information exchange (electronic messaging) standards. Thirteen respondents reported a certification process that requires adherence to national standards for clinical terminology and 13 reported certifying vendors for adherence to requirements or standards for national EHR interoperability.

While not a national certification of software vendors, reimbursement for medical expenditures requires that providers follow certain terminology and exchange requirements in Israel. In Luxembourg, there is a national labelling process for software vendors to access the national EHR system. In Italy, there are no national requirements for certification, but individual regions may impose requirements. In Slovenia, certification has been legally authorised, but it is not yet implemented due to resource constraints. However, to connect to the national EHR system in Slovenia, vendors must use nationally standardised APIs (Application Programming Interfaces).

Table 2.7. Certification requirements of vendors of EHR system software

Respondent	Conform to particular clinical terminology standards	Conform to particular electronic messaging standards	Conform to national e-HR interoperability requirements or standards
Australia	No	Yes	No
Belgium	Yes	Yes	Yes
Canada	No	Yes	Yes[1]
Costa Rica	No	No	No
Czech Republic	No	No	No
Denmark	Yes	Yes	Yes
Estonia	No	No	No
Finland	Yes	Yes	Yes
Germany	n.r.	n.r.	n.r.
Hungary	Yes	Yes	Yes
Iceland	No	No	No
Israel	No	No	No
Italy	No	No	No
Japan	Yes	Yes	Yes
Korea	Yes	Yes	Yes
Lithuania	No	No	No
Luxembourg	No	No	No
Mexico	n.r.	n.r.	n.r.
Netherlands	Yes	Yes	No
Norway	No	No	No
Portugal	Yes[3]	Yes[3]	Yes[3]
Russian Federation	Yes	Yes	Yes
Slovenia	yes	yes	Yes
Sweden	No	Yes	No
Switzerland	Yes[2]	Yes[2]	Yes[2]
Turkey	Yes	Yes	Yes
United States	Yes[4]	Yes[4]	Yes[4]
Total yes	12	15	12

Notes: n.r. Not Reported // n.a. Not Applicable // d.k. Unknown.
1. Optional.
2. Certification of communities using EHR software.
3. E-prescription services are certified.
4. Certification is voluntary but required for reimbursement of medical claims from national insurance programmes (Medicare, Medicaid).
Source: OECD 2021 Survey of Electronic Health Record System Development, Use and Governance.

Auditing clinical records for quality

Another mechanism to verify if health data meet national expectations for data quality is to conduct audits of clinical records. In the 2021 EHR survey, 13 respondents reported that the electronic records of physicians, medical specialists and hospitals are audited to verify quality. An additional three respondents indicated that at least one of these three groups are audited to verify quality. In most cases, it is a national authority that is responsible for undertaking quality audits. In Canada and Sweden, regional authorities conduct audits. In Switzerland, private sector organisations can be certified to then conduct audits as part of certifying the compliance of communities to national requirements including auditing clinical records for quality. Under law in the United States, health care providers are responsible for generating auditing reports on the quality of their clinical records and ensuring data quality.

Table 2.8. Auditing clinical records for quality

Respondent	Physicians	Medical specialists	Hospitals	All
Australia	Yes	Yes	Yes	Yes
Belgium	No	No	Yes	Yes
Canada	Yes	Yes	Yes	Yes
Costa Rica	Yes	Yes	Yes	Yes
Czech Republic	No	No	No	No
Denmark	Yes	Yes	n.r.	Yes
Estonia	No	No	No	No
Finland	n.r.	n.r.	n.r.	n.r.
Germany	n.r.	n.r.	n.r.	n.r.
Hungary	Yes	Yes	Yes	Yes
Iceland	Yes	Yes	Yes	Yes
Israel	Yes	Yes	Yes	Yes
Italy	n.r.	n.r.	n.r.	n.r.
Japan	n.r.	n.r.	n.r.	n.r.
Korea	No	No	No	No
Lithuania	No	No	No	No
Luxembourg	No	No	No	No
Mexico	Yes	Yes	Yes	Yes
Netherlands	Yes	Yes	Yes	Yes
Norway	n.r.	n.r.	n.r.	n.r.
Portugal	Yes	n.r.	Yes	n.r.
Russian Federation	Yes	Yes	Yes	Yes
Slovenia	No	No	No	No
Sweden	Yes	Yes	Yes	Yes
Switzerland	Yes	Yes	Yes	Yes
Turkey	Yes	Yes	Yes	Yes
United States	Yes	Yes	Yes	Yes
Total yes	15	14	15	13

Note: n.r. Not Reported // n.a. Not Applicable // d.k. Unknown.
Source: OECD 2021 Survey of Electronic Health Record System Development, Use and Governance.

Policy levers used by OECD countries to increase EHR interoperability and data use

In 2021, OECD countries reported several different policy levers supporting EHR interoperability and the increased use of data from within EHR systems for direct care, patient centred services, research, statistics, applications development and other uses within the public interest. This section reviews countries use of laws or regulations requiring data standards; certification of software vendors; and incentive payments.

In 2021, 13 countries reported implementing laws or regulations that require health care providers to adopt electronic health record systems that meet national standards for both clinical terminology and electronic messaging (data exchange).

Sixteen countries reported laws or regulations requiring health care providers to meet standards for national EHR interoperability. In Iceland, regulations require that health care providers can connect to the Icelandic HealthNet (national EHR network). In Italy, the law defines a national federated system with a mandatory, nationwide, interoperability. In Lithuania, data is structured and standardised by law and must be suitable to be forwarded smoothly to the ESPBI IS (central EHR system). In Luxembourg, connecting to the DSP (central EHR system) requires meeting legal requirements for data standardisation. In Slovenia, IHE XDS and OpenEHR standards are required with proprietary modifications that are set out in law. In Switzerland, certifying communities and software vendors are required to meet national standards including HL7 FHIR and IHE. In Portugal, by law, health care providers IT systems must conform to a catalogue of standards to exchange data.

Table 2.9. Laws or regulations requiring adoption and standardisation of electronic health records

Respondent	Laws or regulations require clinical terminology standards	Laws or regulations require electronic messaging standards	Laws or regulations require health care providers meet standards for national EHR interoperability
Australia	No	No	No
Belgium	No	No	No
Canada	n.r.	n.r.	n.r.
Costa Rica	Yes	Yes	Yes
Czech Republic	n.r.	n.r.	n.r.
Denmark	No	No	Yes
Estonia	Yes	Yes	Yes
Finland	Yes	Yes	Yes
Germany	n.r.	n.r.	n.r.
Hungary	Yes	Yes	Yes
Iceland	Yes	Yes[1]	Yes
Israel	Yes[2]	No	No
Italy	Yes	Yes	Yes
Japan	Yes	Yes	Yes
Korea	Yes	Yes	Yes
Lithuania	Yes	Yes	Yes
Luxembourg	No	Yes	Yes
Mexico	n.r.	n.r.	n.r.
Netherlands	Yes	No	No
Norway	n.r.	n.r.	Yes
Portugal	No	Yes	No
Russian Federation	Yes	Yes	Yes
Slovenia	Yes	Yes	Yes
Sweden	n.r.	n.r.	n.r.
Switzerland	Yes	Yes	Yes
Turkey	Yes	Yes	Yes
United States	n.a.	n.a.	n.a.
Total yes	15	15	16

Note: n.r. Not Reported // n.a. Not Applicable // d.k. Unknown.
1. Law recommends the use of EHRs.
2. For diagnosis.
Source: OECD 2021 Survey of Electronic Health Record System Development, Use and Governance.

Another policy lever is requiring vendors of electronic health records systems to be certified to be in conformance with national data standards. Overall, 13 countries have a software vendor certification that requires vendors to meet national standards for both clinical terminology and electronic messaging.

Table 2.10. Certification requirements of EHR software vendors

Respondent	Conform to particular clinical terminology standards	Conform to particular electronic messaging standards	Conform to standards or requirements for national e-HR interoperability	Standards or requirements vendors must meet to be certified
Australia	No	Yes	No	There is a mix of CDA and FHIR capability implemented and moving to use FHIR predominately
Belgium	Yes	Yes	Yes	https://www.ehealth.fgov.be/ehealthplatform/fr/service-enregistrement-des-logiciels
Canada	No	Yes	Yes[1]	https://www.infoway-inforoute.ca/en/our-partners/industry/vendor-certification-services
Costa Rica	n.r.	n.r.	n.r.	
Czech Republic	n.r.	n.r.	n.r.	
Denmark	Yes	Yes	Yes	National shared document standards with some connection to IHE and HL7 schemas
Estonia	n.r.	n.r.	n.r.	
Finland	Yes	Yes	Yes	Detailed specifications, including terminology standards and implementation guides
Germany	n.r.	n.r.	n.r.	
Hungary	Yes	Yes	Yes	EESZT API specification and EESZT-related regulations to join to the EESZT
Iceland	n.r.	n.r.	n.r.	
Israel	n.r.	n.r.	n.r.	
Italy	n.r.	n.r.	n.r.	
Japan	Yes	Yes	Yes	Japanese standard disease code and lab test code master
Korea	Yes	Yes	Yes	
Lithuania	n.r.	n.r.	n.r.	
Luxembourg	No	No	No	
Mexico	n.r.	n.r.	n.r.	
Netherlands	Yes	Yes	No	
Norway	n.r.	n.r.	n.r.	
Portugal	Yes	Yes	Yes	
Russian Federation	Yes	Yes	Yes	
Slovenia	Yes	Yes	Yes	National standards to participate in EHR exchange
Sweden	No	Yes	No	National agreed standards by SALAR/Inera
Switzerland	Yes	Yes	Yes	https://www.e-health-suisse.ch/technik-semantik/epd-projectathon/programmierhilfen-epd/relevante-spezifikationen.html. HL7/FHIR/IHE, partly national adaptation of IHE integration profiles. Semantics: SNOMED CT
Turkey	Yes	Yes	Yes	Dokuman Online, SKRS, VEM, all are defined by MoH, former two defining data collection standards while the latter one defines data transfer standard between products from different vendors
United States	Yes	Yes	Yes	US government's ONC Health IT Certification Program must conform to the full scope of the product's required capabilities, including regulatory/conformance expectation clarifications and interpretations set forth in Certification Companion Guides. For a full list of vendor certification criteria including conformance and standards required by criteria see: https://www.healthit.gov/topic/certification-ehrs/2015-edition-cures-update-test-method
Total yes	13	16	13	

Note: n.r. Not Reported // n.a. Not Applicable // d.k. Unknown.
1. Optional.
Source: OECD 2021 Survey of Electronic Health Record System Development, Use and Governance.

Finally, 8 countries have incentive payments or penalties for health care providers to install EHR systems from a certified software vendor, 9 have these payments to health care providers to keep EHR systems up-to-date regarding changes to national standards over time and 11 have incentives or penalties to meet national requirements for EHR interoperability.

Table 2.11. Incentives or penalties to install EHR systems from a certified vendor, to keep standards up-to-date and to meet national interoperability requirements

Respondent	Incentives or penalties to install electronic record systems from a certified vendor	Incentives or penalties to keep the EHR system up-to-date as terminology and electronic messaging standards change over time	Incentives or penalties to adopt standards or other requirements for national e-HR interoperability	Description of incentives or penalties
Australia	No	No	Yes	The Practice Incentives Program eHealth Incentive (ePIP) aims to encourage general practices to keep up to date with the latest developments in digital health. In order to meet ePIP requirements, practices are expected to adopt compliant software for secure messaging and the My Health Record system and make use of e-prescribing and nationally recognised disease classification or terminology system.
Belgium	Yes	Yes	Yes	As a general practitioner you are eligible for an integrated premium to support the practice and the use of E-services (= integrated practice premium). You must then meet a number of conditions.
Canada	No	No	No	
Costa Rica	No	No	No	
Czech Republic	No	No	No	
Denmark	No	No	no	We have incentives and penalties that are not in use, but yearly economic agreements regulate the requirements as well as the annual fiscal agreement.
Estonia	No	No	Yes	Data exchange between EHNIS and health providers is a mandatory requirement in the health service reimbursement contract between the Estonian Health Insurance Fund and health care providers..
Finland	Yes	Yes	Yes	Legislation, decrees and rules, referring to more detailed specifications, and mandates for supervisory authorities (other organisations) to enforce compliance.
Germany	n.r.	n.r.	n.r.	
Hungary	Yes	Yes	Yes	The health care provider is bound to fulfill legal rules. National Authority can audit and investigate the adherence of rules. In cases of non-compliance, consequences can be warning, penalty or withdrawal of licence.
Iceland	No	No	No and Yes[2]	Primary health care clinics receive a refund based on the usage of the national patient portal.
Israel	No	No	No	
Italy	No	Yes	Yes	Regions receive specific funds in order to implement the EHR according to defined objectives. Every year Regions are evaluated to verify their performance in providing health care services within the National Health Service. Among the indicators, the availability of specific EHR functionalities are included.
Japan	Yes	Yes	Yes	Health care providers that introduce a standardised e-HR system can receive a subsidy from the fund to support digitalisation of medical information. In addition, in the medical fee system, health care providers are evaluated regarding providing medical information using the standards.
Korea	No	No	No	
Lithuania	No	No	No	
Luxembourg	No	No[1]	No	
Mexico	n.r.	n.r.	n.r.	
Netherlands	Yes	Yes	No	Financial penalty; no incentives
Norway	No	No	No	
Portugal	No	No	No	

Respondent	Incentives or penalties to install electronic record systems from a certified vendor	Incentives or penalties to keep the EHR system up-to-date as terminology and electronic messaging standards change over time	Incentives or penalties to adopt standards or other requirements for national e-HR interoperability	Description of incentives or penalties
Russian Federation	n.r.	n.r.	n.r.	
Slovenia	Yes	No	n.r.	Major upgrades of hospital information systems are co-financed, e.g. via joint projects with software vendors
Sweden	No	No	No	
Switzerland	No	Yes	Yes	
Turkey	Yes	No	Yes	
United States	Yes	Yes	Yes	The US Government has programs such as the Promoting Interoperability Program which provides incentives to health care providers to adopt certified electronic health record technology. As previously noted, these incentives are voluntary for providers participating in the major US public health insurance programs who benefit from payment incentives as a result of meeting programme requirements regarding the use of certified health IT. For more information see: https://www.cms.gov/Regulations-and-Guidance/Legislation/EHRIncentivePrograms/Basics. Additionally, federal laws penalise vendors that engage in information blocking practices or fail to comply with certification programme requirement. Penalties may include decertification and/or civil monetary penalties. For more information on information blocking requirements see: https://www.healthit.gov/topic/information-blocking.
Total yes	8	9	11	

Note: n.r. Not Reported // n.a. Not Applicable // d.k. Unknown.
1. National terminology referential bases are put in place and maintained by Agence eSanté.
2. Incentive for primary health care clinics to use the national patient portal.
Source: OECD 2021 Survey of Electronic Health Record System Development, Use and Governance.

Patient portal to their own medical records

In most countries, patients have access to and can interact with their own medical records within a secure Internet portal. 'Access' means patients can view information contained in their own record and 'interact' means that patients can amend information, upload data or interact with their health care provider. Thirteen countries reported that 100% of patients have access to their own medical records through an Internet portal and 12 reported that 100% of patients can interact with their portal. Eighteen countries reported that patients can view their own records from all of their current health care providers and containing their current medications, lab tests, and imaging results.

Table 2.12. Patient access to and interaction with their own EHR through a secure Internet portal

Respondent	Patients can access their EHR via a secure Internet portal (Patient Portal)	Proportion of patients who can access	Patients view their own records from ALL of their current health care providers and containing their current medications, laboratory tests, imaging results within the Patient Portal	Patients can interact with the patient Internet Portal	Proportion of patients who can interact
Australia	Yes	90%	Yes[4]	Yes	0%
Belgium	Yes	80%	No	No	0%
Canada[1]	Yes	27%	No	d.k.	d.k.
Costa Rica	Yes	33%	No	Yes	33%
Czech Republic[5]	Yes	15%	No	Yes	8%
Denmark	Yes	100%	Yes	Yes	100%
Estonia	Yes	100%	Yes	No	n.a
Finland	Yes	100%	No	Yes	100%
Germany	Yes	100%	Yes	Yes	target: 100%
Hungary	Yes	40%	Yes	No	0%
Iceland	Yes	100%	No	Yes	100%
Israel	Yes	100%	Most	No	100%
Italy	Yes	100%	Yes	Yes	100%
Japan	Yes	100%	Yes	No	100%
Korea	No	n.a.	n.a.	n.a.	n.a.
Lithuania	Yes	100%	Yes	Yes	100%
Luxembourg	Yes	100%	Yes	Yes	n.a.
Mexico	No	n.a.	n.a	n.a	n.a
Netherlands	Yes	75%	Yes	Yes	20%
Norway	No	n.a.	n.a	n.a	n.a
Portugal	Yes	25%	No	Yes	25%
Russian Federation	Yes	100%	Yes	Yes	100%
Slovenia	Yes	5%	Yes	Yes[3]	None
Sweden	Yes	100%	Yes[6]	Yes	100%
Switzerland	Yes	n.r	Yes	Yes[2]	100%[2]
Turkey	Yes	100%	Yes	Yes	100%
United States	Yes	51%	No	Yes	n.a.
Total yes	24		16	18	

Note: n.r. Not Reported // n.a. Not Applicable // d.k. Unknown.
1. Regional (state/province) level differences.
2. All patients can upload PDF files to the portal.
3. To some extent.
4. When providers upload files to the national system.
5. Two regions and certain hospitals.
6. Some private providers not included.
Source: OECD 2021 Survey of Electronic Health Record System Development, Use and Governance.

Secondary analysis of EHR system data

Most respondents are regularly extracting data from the EHR system for public health monitoring (16 countries). Such uses have been accelerating in response to the COVID-19 pandemic. Further, countries have been increasingly depending upon data with EHR systems for their superior timeliness, enabling analysis of the pandemic situation and response in near real time. Ten countries reported regularly extracting EHR data to monitor the performance of the health system including, treatments, costs and health outcomes. Twelve countries regularly rely upon EHR data to monitor patient safety, including post-market surveillance of medications. Ten countries report that EHR data are extracted for health and medical research to improve patient care, health system efficiency or population health, such as long-term follow-up studies of patients experiencing different risk factors, health conditions and treatments. Five countries are regularly relying upon EHR data to facilitate and contribute to clinical trials, such as following clinical cohorts to measure health outcomes and health care encounters over time. Five countries also enable physicians to query the data to inform themselves about previous treatments and treatment outcomes when caring for patients.

Table 2.13. Regular secondary analysis of EHR system data

Respondent	Public health monitoring	Monitoring health system performance	Monitoring patient safety	Facilitating and contributing to clinical trials	Supporting physician treatment decisions	Research to improve patient care, health system efficiency or population health
Australia	No	No	No	No	No	No
Belgium	Yes	Yes	Yes	d.k.	No	Yes
Canada	No	No	No	No	No	No
Costa Rica	Yes	Yes	Yes	Yes	No	Yes
Czech Republic	Yes	Yes	No	No	No	No
Denmark	Yes	Yes	Yes	Yes	Yes	Yes
Estonia	Yes	No	Yes	No	No	No
Finland	Yes	Yes	Yes	No	No	Yes
Germany	n.r.	n.r.	n.r.	n.r.	n.r.	Yes
Hungary	Yes	No	No	No	No	No
Iceland	Yes	No	Yes	No	Yes, partly[1]	Yes
Israel	Yes	No	Yes	No	No	Yes
Italy	No	No	No	No	No	No
Japan	Yes	n.r.	Yes	Yes	n.r.	n.r.
Korea	No	No	No	No	No	No
Lithuania	Yes	Yes	Yes	No	No	No
Luxembourg	No	No	No	No	No	No
Mexico	No	No	No	No	No	No
Netherlands	Yes	Yes	Yes	No	Yes	Yes
Norway	n.r.	n.r.	n.r.	n.r.	n.r.	n.r.
Portugal	Yes	Yes	d.k.	No	No	No
Russian Federation	n.r.	n.r.	n.r.	n.r.	n.r.	n.r.
Slovenia	Yes	n.r.	n.r.	n.r.	n.r.	n.r.
Sweden	Yes	Yes	Yes	Yes	Yes	Yes
Switzerland	No	No	No	No	No	No
Turkey	Yes	Yes	Yes	Yes	Yes	Yes
United States	No	No	No	No	No	No
Total yes	16	10	12	5	5	10

Note: n.r. Not Reported // n.a. Not Applicable // d.k. Unknown.
1. Physicians can query their own data.
Source: OECD 2021 Survey of Electronic Health Record System Development, Use and Governance.

Development of artificial intelligence algorithms, machine learning and analytics

The Netherlands, Denmark and Israel are the three countries with the most applications of machine learning, artificial intelligence algorithm development and other more advanced analytics based on EHR data that were measured in the 2021 survey. Overall, 8 countries reported data mining to find or extract data from the EHR; 8 countries are using EHRs to develop messages and alerts for patient care or managerial decision-making; and 7 countries are using EHRs to develop predictive analytics trained on EHR data for patient care or managerial decision-making. Six countries report national projects to integrate or link EHR data with genomic, environmental, behavioural, economic or other data. Three countries are also using natural language processing to convert free text to standardised (coded) data.

Table 2.14. Machine learning, artificial intelligence and analytics with EHR system data

Respondent	Data mining to find or extract data from the EHR system	Natural language processing to convert text based data to coded data	Automated alerts and messages for patient care or managerial decision-making	Predictive analytics for patient care or managerial decision-making (trained on EHR data)	Other applications of machine learning/AI developed with EHR system data	National projects to integrate or link EHR data with genomic, environmental, behavioural, economic or other data
Australia	No	No	No	No	No	No
Belgium	No	No	No	No	No	Yes
Canada	No	No	No	No	No	No
Costa Rica	Yes	No	Yes	Yes	No	No
Czech Republic	No	No	No	No	No	No
Denmark	Yes	Yes	Yes	Yes	Yes	No
Estonia	No	No	Yes	No	No	Yes
Finland	Yes	No	Yes	No	n.r.	No
Germany	No	No	n.r.	No	n.r.	Yes
Hungary	No	No	No	No	No	No
Iceland	No	No	Yes	No	No	No
Israel	Yes	Yes	Yes	Yes	Yes	Yes
Italy	No	No	No	No	No	Yes
Japan	n.r.	n.r.	n.r.	n.r.	n.r.	No
Korea	No	No	No	No	No	No
Lithuania	No	No	No	No	No	No
Luxembourg	Yes[2]	No[1]	No	Yes[2]	No	No
Mexico	No	No	No	No	No	No
Netherlands	Yes	Yes	Yes	Yes	Yes	Yes
Norway	n.r.	n.r.	n.r.	n.r.	n.r.	n.r.
Portugal	Yes	No	No	Yes	Yes	No
Russian Federation	n.r.	n.r.	n.r.	n.r.	n.r.	n.r.
Slovenia	No	No	No	No	No	No
Sweden	No	No	Yes	Yes	No	No
Switzerland	No	No	No	No	No	No
Turkey	Yes	No	No	No	No	No
United States	No	No	No	No	No	No
Total yes	8	3	8	7	4	6

Note: n.r. Not Reported // n.a. Not Applicable // d.k. Unknown.
1. Physicians can query their own data.
2. In development as part of the creation of a data lake.
Source: OECD 2021 Survey of Electronic Health Record System Development, Use and Governance.

Summary of the situation across the OECD regarding the interoperability of EHR systems

In 2021, most OECD countries surveyed had: 1. established a **national organisation** that was responsible for setting national clinical terminology and electronic messaging (exchange) standards; 2. created a **multidisciplinary governing body** for the national organisation that represents key stakeholders; 3. use **unique identification** of patients and health care providers; 4. adopted **international terminology standards** for diagnoses, medications, laboratory tests and medical images; 5 adopted the **HL7 FHIR standard** for data exchange (electronic messaging); and participate in **global collaborative projects** to improve international data standards.

Most countries have one **country-wide electronic health record system** and are exchanging EHRs at the national level including data sharing among physician offices and hospitals about patients' treatment, medication use, laboratory tests and images.

Most countries have a **Patient Internet Portal** where patients can access their own medical records from all of their current health care providers. Most are extracting data from their EHR system for **public health monitoring**. Many countries are also utilising EHRs for other secondary purposes including health system **performance monitoring**, patient safety **surveillance** and health and medical **research**. Some are also developing **big data analytics** including machine learning, artificial intelligence algorithms with EHRs.

Countries reported several levers to improve the spread and interoperability of their electronic clinical data.

- Sixteen had a **legal requirement** for health care providers to meet national standards for EHR interoperability and 13 had a legal requirement for health care providers to adopt an electronic health record system (software) that conformed with national standards for both clinical terminology and electronic messaging (exchange).
- Thirteen countries had a **certification of eHR system (software) vendors** that required them to adopt national standards for both clinical terminology and electronic messaging and 13 had a certification that required software vendors to meet requirements for national EHR interoperability.
- Eleven countries had **financial incentives** (or penalties) for health care providers to install an EHR system that meets national standards and requirements for national EHR interoperability. Nine countries report incentives for health care providers to keep their EHR system up-to-date as clinical terminology and electronic messaging standards change over time; and 8 reported incentives for health care providers to install and EHR system from a certified software vendor.

References

Cavoukian, A. (2006), *Privacy By Design: The Seven Foundational Principles*, IAPP Resource Centre, https://iapp.org/media/pdf/resource_center/pbd_implement_7found_principles.pdf. [9]

CPME (2021), *CPME Policy on the European Health Data Space*, CPME 2021/097 FINAL, https://www.cpme.eu/index.php?downloadunprotected=/uploads/adopted/2021/3/CPME_AD_Board_20032021_097.FINAL_.CPME_.Policy.on_.EU_.health.data_.space_.pdf. [7]

EC (2021), *European Health Data Space*, https://ec.europa.eu/health/ehealth/dataspace_en. [5]

EC (2021a), *e-Health Digital Health and Care - European Health Data Space*, https://ec.europa.eu/health/ehealth/dataspace_en. [6]

EMA (2021), *DARWIN EU Coordination Centre, Technical specifications for competitive procedure with negotiation*, EMA/128740/2021, https://www.ema.europa.eu/en/about-us/how-we-work/big-data/data-analysis-real-world-interrogation-network-darwin-eu.   [8]

Institute of Medicine (2004), "Health Care Data Standards", in *Patient Safety: Achieving a New Standard for Care*, National Academies Press, Washington, D.C., http://dx.doi.org/10.17226/10863.   [3]

Magazanik, L. (forthcoming), *Supporting Health Innovation With Fair Information Practice Principles: Key issues emerging from the OECD-Israel Workshop of 19-20 January 2021*, OECD.   [11]

Oderkirk, J. (2021), "Survey results: National health data infrastructure and governance", *OECD Health Working Papers*, No. 127, OECD Publishing, Paris, https://doi.org/10.1787/55d24b5d-en.   [10]

Open Data Institute (n.d.), *What is data Infrastructure*, https://theodi.org/topic/data-infrastructure/.   [2]

Schulz, S., R. Stegwee and C. Chronaki (2018), "Standards in Healthcare Data", in *Fundamentals of Clinical Data Science*, Springer International Publishing, Cham, http://dx.doi.org/10.1007/978-3-319-99713-1_3.   [4]

Van Driesden G, W. (2021), *Quick Guide to Dutch Healthcare*, De Argumentenfakriek, https://www.argumentenfabriek.nl/products/quickguidedutchhealthcare/.   [1]

Notes

[1] In addition, the **Youth Act**, which regulates assistance provided to children, adolescents and their parents – which is a municipal responsibility. It covers developmental and parenting support for families, psychosocial and psychiatric problems, supplementing what families cannot do themselves.

3 The strengths and weaknesses of the current Dutch way of managing health and social care data

This chapter describes the key strengths and limitations of the Dutch health system in terms of establishing an integrated health information system. It examines key legislation and policies, health data infrastructure and health data interoperability for several purposes including direct patient care, measuring health care quality, developing personal health environments, and enabling research infrastructures for the life sciences and the social sciences. Several key strengths and advantages are identified. But the chapter highlights some of the problems brought about by a fragmented, market-based system for smooth exchange of, and access to, health data for various purposes that are in the public interest. The chapter identifies the need for a generic, co-ordinated policy strategy towards digitalisation that is under the stewardship of the central government and includes a broad array of stakeholder groups in its design and implementation.

The previous chapter outlined the key characteristics of the Dutch health system and how these influence the management and use of data to achieve policy objectives. It described the main features of an integrated health information system in normative and positive terms. It also explained how developments in health data governance and in interoperable electronic health record systems (EHRs) compare across OECD countries and highlighted related European projects.

This chapter examines the main strengths and shortcomings of current arrangements in the Netherlands regarding the establishment of an integrated health information system including legislation and policies, health information infrastructure and health data interoperability. Separate discussions and initiatives are taking place within the Netherlands about the interoperability of clinical data for direct patient care, for measuring health care quality, developing of personal health environments, and about the creation of research infrastructures for the life sciences and the social sciences. But a national effort toward creating an integrated health information system that could modernise patient experiences, support integrated health care delivery, improve monitoring of public health, support evidence-based policy making, and encourage innovations in health technologies and advancements in life sciences and social science research is still mostly absent.

The importance of such a system has recently been highlighted in the Dutch media,[1] which reported difficulties with transferring COVID-19 patients between hospitals because their medical information cannot be exchanged electronically. This results in not only delays and inefficiencies – with busy clinicians having to manually transcribe patients' data from the local electronic record to a CD to send with the patient – but also the risk of subsequent medical errors that manual transcribing of information entails.

Before the elections in the Netherlands in March 2021, the majority of political parties expressed the need for further digitalisation in general and the need to address digitalisation in health care specifically. Following the acceptance of the new law on interoperability of health care data (WEGIZ) in both chambers, follow up plans have been published and discussed in parliament (i.e. letter of the minister of health to parliament of 15 October 2021). The need for a more generic strategy towards digitalisation under the stewardship of government seems to be broadly supported and will likely result in further steps by a new cabinet. At the time of writing, coalition talks between the four parties presently comprising the cabinet are taking place with the intention to reach agreement on programme and composition of a new cabinet.

Several strengths and advantages will enable creating an integrated health information system

Netherlands performed well compared with OECD countries in many aspects of health data maturity, use and governance in the 2019-20 OECD survey discussed in Chapter 2. In most cases, the data needed to achieve an integrated health information system and fulfil the government's policy objectives exist. All that is needed are a set of consistent rules to connect actors in the information system together and to enable access to the right data by the right people at the right time.

Expert consultations revealed other strengths. For example, patient engagement and leadership of patient groups toward data interoperability is strong in the Netherlands. Significant progress has been made in developing data exchange standards. The Informatieberaad Zorg (IB) has made good progress in advancing the case for data exchange for better care delivery, although the IB is a voluntary body with no legal status or funding and its membership and focus is limited to primary users and use of health data.

The Dutch Erasmus University MC leads the development of an open science federated network of data providers in Europe called the European Health Data & Evidence Network (EHDEN) that are coding health and health care data to the global Observational Medical Outcomes Partnership (OMOP) common data model (EHDEN, 2021[1]). The CBS provides an example of good practice, but its limited remit prevents it from working actively in the health space. Two Dutch initiatives – ODDISSEI and Health RI – exhibit the right characteristics to promote better data management for secondary purposes.

In addition, the Netherlands has a unique 'can-do' culture with a strong tradition of finding solutions to seemingly intractable problems. This has often relied on striking a balance between individual liberty and the need for collective action (it is, after all, a country that manages to not only exist but thrive below sea level).

An example of local innovation in this context is the personal health train – an important technology developed in the Netherlands, which can enable data exchange on a distributed/federated network thus avoiding the need for central aggregation of personal data (Dutch Tech Centre for Life Sciences, 2021[2]). Similarly, the EHDEN project is a federated network that avoids the need for central aggregation of personal data.

Data custodians in the Netherlands adopt different approaches to health data governance and exchange

The Netherlands' health data landscape is characterised by the highest number of data custodians reported in the OECD. This fragmented structure does not preclude being able to leverage available data to achieve the objectives listed earlier. It does, however, create greater challenges to data sharing and integration than in other countries.

A 2019/20 OECD survey found that most OECD countries have 3 to 5 custodians of the 13 national health and health care datasets considered integral to a national health information system. Custodians of these data are usually national governmental organisations such as health ministries, national statistical offices or health information agencies funded by the government (Oderkirk, 2021[3]).

The Netherlands reported nine separate custodians of key national data sets, with only one custodian being a fully governmental body, the CBS. Most data custodians are either government-funded autonomous foundations or institutes, or private-sector funded non-profit organisations (Table 3.1).

Dutch health data custodians adopt different approaches to health data governance, including policies around data sharing and access to data for within-country and cross-border statistical and research projects (Table 3.2 and Table 3.3). Further, their adoption of best practices to protect privacy and data security, including 'privacy-by-design' varies.

The lack of a Common Data Model for health and related social and socio-economic data, as well as a common data governance framework for data exchange, dataset linkage and integration, translates into each instance where data need to be integrated across different organisations becoming a separate project requiring a great deal of effort to standardise data elements, develop governance arrangements, seek approval for data sharing and integration and so on. In new data integration projects, the majority of funding and human effort is taken up by these preliminary steps and the analytical and publication steps are a minority of the effort.

Nonetheless, the Netherlands conducts projects on a regular basis that require record linkage across key national health datasets. The key national health datasets investigated by the OECD in 2019-20 include hospital and mental hospital in-patients, emergency care, primary care, prescription medicines, cancer, diabetes and CVD registries, long-term care, population health survey, patient-experiences survey and mortality data.

With the strong flow of health care data to the Netherlands CBS, the Netherlands is among a minority of OECD countries who regularly link health and health care data to a rich set of contextual data about risk factors, living conditions, socio-economic status and demographic data. Population registry (demographic) data are linked with hospital inpatient, mental hospital inpatient, primary care, cancer registry, long-term care, mortality and population health survey data. Tax data (income) are linked to hospital inpatient, long-term care and population health survey data. Quality of life questionnaire data are linked to cancer registry data.

However, there are key datasets in the Netherlands that are not regularly linked and that are crucial to understanding health trajectories and outcomes including national data on prescription medicines as well as data within the national cardiovascular disease and diabetes registries and data on patients in emergency health care.

Table 3.1. Custodians of the Netherlands key national health datasets

Key National Health Dataset	Dataset Custodian
Hospital in-patient data	Dutch Hospital Data (DHD) + CBS
Mental hospital In-patient data	NZa (Nederlandse Zorgauthoriteit)
Emergency health care data	Veiligheid NL (Consumer and Safety Institute)
Primary care data	Nivel (Nederlands Instituut voor Onderzoek van de Gezondheidszorg)
Prescription medicines data	Zorginstituut Nederland (ZiN)
Cancer registry data	Netherlands Comprehensive Cancer Organisation (IKNL)
Diabetes registry data	DPARD (Dutch Pediatric and Adult Registry of Diabetes)
Cardio-vascular disease registry	Nederlande Hart Registratie (Dutch Heart Registration)
Mortality Data	CBS (Centraal Bureau voor de Statistiek)
Formal long-term care data	Several organisations (CIZ, Het CAK, NZa, ZIN, SVB, Bureau Jeugdzorg, Vektis)
Patient experiences survey data	n.a.
Population health survey data	CBS (Centraal Bureau voor de Statistiek)
Population Census/Registry data	CBS (Centraal Bureau voor de Statistiek)

Source: OECD 2019-20 Survey of Health Data Development, Use and Governance. See Oderkirk (2021[3]), "Survey results: National health data infrastructure and governance", https://doi.org/10.1787/55d24b5d-en.

Table 3.2. Sharing and access to de-identified data varies by health dataset custodian

Analysts from the following organisations could be approved access to de-identified data for statistical or research purposes in the public interest

	Hospital in-patient data	Mental hospital in-patient data	Emergency health care data	Primary care data	Prescription medicines data	Cancer registry data	Diabetes registry data	Cardio-vascular disease registry data	Mortality data	Formal long-term care data	% of national health care datasets
Government ministry or government national data custodian	Yes	Yes	No	Yes	Yes	Yes	No	Yes	Yes	Yes	80%
University or non-profit research institute	Yes	No	Yes	Yes	Yes	Yes	No	Yes	Yes	Yes	80%
Health Care Provider	Yes	No	Yes	Yes	Yes	Yes	Yes	Yes	No	No	70%
For-profit business	No	No	No	No	Yes	No	No	Yes	No	No	20%
Foreign university or non-profit research institute	No	No	Yes	Yes	Yes	Yes	No	Yes	Yes	No	60%

Source: OECD 2019-20 Survey of Health Data Development, Use and Governance. See Oderkirk (2021[3]), "Survey results: National health data infrastructure and governance", https://doi.org/10.1787/55d24b5d-en.

Table 3.3. Data protection and security policies and practices vary by dataset custodian

	Hospital in-patient data	Mental hospital in-patient data	Emergency health care data	Primary care data	Prescription medicines data	Cancer registry data	Diabetes registry data	Cardio-vascular disease registry data	Mortality data	Formal long-term care data	% of national health care datasets
Legislation authorises dataset creation	Yes	Yes	No	Yes	Yes	No	Yes	Yes	Yes	Yes[2]	80%
Data Protection officer	Yes	Yes	Yes	Yes	Yes	Yes	Yes	Yes	Yes[2]	Yes	100%
Control and tracking of staff data access	Yes	Yes	No	No	No	Yes	Yes	No	Yes	Yes	60%
Process to assess risk of data re-identification	Yes	Yes	No	Yes	No	Yes	No	Yes	Yes	Yes	70%
Treatment of variables posing a reidentification risk	Yes	Yes	Yes	Yes	No	Yes	Yes	No	Yes	Yes	80%
Public description of the dataset including its legal basis	Yes	No	Yes	Yes	Yes	n.r.	Yes	Yes	Yes	No	70%
Sharing data with external researchers is legally authorised	Yes	Yes	No	Yes	Yes	No	Yes	No	Yes	Yes	70%
Individuals consent or opt-out to data sharing	No	Opt-out	Opt-out	Opt-out	Consent	No	Opt-out	No	Consent/ opt-out	Consent	70%
Procedure to request access to data and approval criteria are public	Yes	Yes	No	Yes	No	Yes	Yes	Yes	Yes	Yes	80%
Procedure to request a dataset linkage and approval criteria are public	n.a.	Yes	No	Yes	No	Yes	No	Yes	Yes	Yes	60%
Approval body for dataset linkages	n.a.	n.r.	Veiligheid NL (Consumer and Safety Institute)	GPs and privacy committee	n.r.	n.a.	n.a.	Board of directors	Central Bureau of Statistics	Health care insurers	50%
Standard data sharing agreement	Yes	Yes	Yes	Yes	Yes	Yes	Yes	Yes	Yes	Yes	100%
Secure remote data access service	Yes	Yes	No	No	No	No	No	Yes	Yes	No	40%
Supervised research data centre	No	No	No	No	No	No	No	Yes	Yes	Yes	30%

Source: OECD 2019-20 Survey of Health Data Development, Use and Governance. See Oderkirk (2021[3]), "Survey results: National health data infrastructure and governance", https://doi.org/10.1787/55d24b5d-en.

Legislation, regulations and their interpretation can hinder data exchange

In their submission to the 2019-20 OECD survey, Dutch officials reported that organisations can create datasets and can undertake dataset linkages only if their proposed activities meet the requirements of the *EU General Data Protection Regulation* (GDPR) and the *Medical Treatment Act*. The Netherlands' Data Protection Authority evaluates whether datasets meet GDPR requirements.

However, without national health data governance guidelines for the implementation of the GDPR, officials reported that dataset custodians each have their own interpretation of the GDPR and that some have interpreted the GDPR as indicating that past data exchange arrangements are no longer legally permitted. For example, sharing data between custodians for the purpose of calculating indicators of health care outcomes by health care institution is often considered legally prohibited.

The current approach reduces benefits while increasing risks to data privacy

A fragmented approach to health data management creates (a) missed opportunities to generate improvements in health and other desirable outcomes, and (b) heightened risk of personal health data being compromised. A recent example of a potentially preventable health data privacy breach was due to an absence of stronger security requirements on institutions handling personal health data and resulted in attempts to sell individuals' COVID-19 status on the dark web (see Box 3.1).

Box 3.1. COVID-19 data breach could have been avoided by stronger governance

In February 2021 there were local and international media reports of a large breach of personal health data from the systems of the Gemeentelijke gezondheidsdienst (GGD). The GGD is responsible for COVID-19 testing and vaccinations. Media reports and experts interviewed by the OECD indicated that there was a lack of safeguards including a lack of staff data access controls, gaps in the tracking of staff data access, inadequate supervision of data protection, inadequate staff training in data protection, and a lack of system-level data protection against the risk of data downloading.

A strong, national data governance framework, with requirements for data custodians to adopt and maintain a privacy-by-design approach to their IT systems and with the controls and safeguards required of data custodians that are set out in the OECD Recommendation on Health Data Governance, may well have limited or avoided the egregious data breach (see Annex B). For example, the OECD Recommendation in Article 12 sets out safeguards to be implemented within health data custodians including lines of accountability, data privacy and security training for all staff members, formal risk management processes, and technological, organisational and physical measures designed to protect privacy and data security.

Source: Loohuis (2021[4]), "Data of Thousands of Dutch Citizens Leaked from Government COVID-19 Systems", https://www.computerweekly.com/news/252495983/Data-of-thousands-of-Dutch-citizens-leaked-from-government-Covid-19-systems.

Privacy-protected data uses are supported by the GDPR but need to be implemented

Implementation of the GDPR can include national legislations regarding the collection, exchange, linkage and accessibility of health data and authorisation of data processing by a legal basis that is not limited to patient consent. Implementation guidelines for organisations processing health data are also necessary to avoid divergent interpretations that unnecessarily reduce data exchange and collaboration.

A recent preliminary opinion of European Data Protection Supervisor regarding the creation of a European Health Data Space (EHDS) explains that because the space will be created to enhance access to health data in order to allow for evidence-based policy decisions and for scientific research within the EU, they do not consider Article 6(1)(a) GDPR (i.e. consent of the data subject), as the most appropriate legal basis (EDPS, 2020[5]). Instead, they refer to Article 6(1)e that authorises health data processing where processing is necessary for the performance of a task carried out in the public interest or in the exercise of official authority vested in the controller; Article 9(2)(i) that allows processing of sensitive data for reasons of public interest and Article 9(2)(j) that authorises processing operations involving health data when the processing is necessary for scientific research purposes. Further, they explain that Article 89 allows member states to develop legislation that provides for derogations from certain rights, subject to safeguards.

GDPR provisions may still provoke some limitations, however, such as the use of data for exploratory purposes including machine learning and AI algorithm development, which require greater volumes of data than principles of data minimisation may support (Oliveira Hashiguchi, Slawomirski and Oderkirk, 2021[6]). Another example is the use of blockchain technologies which can violate rights set out in the GDPR, such as the right to erasure (OECD, 2020[7]). Resolving these issues will require further work at the European level but do not limit the Netherlands from adopting the recommendations set out in this report.

Both a national health data governance framework and guidance on the implementation of the GDPR would help to overcome different legal interpretations that are limiting data sharing in the Netherlands. It is therefore encouraging to hear of discussions about legislation governing secondary uses of health data have begun. Such laws to enable secure access to personal data for research and other purposes with public benefit have been enacted in other jurisdictions and were discussed in Chapter 2.

A further issue raised by experts in the Netherlands are legacy legislations that precede the GDPR and that may create unnecessary obstacles to the exchange and use of health data. In particular, the Medical Treatment Contracts Act (Wgbo) requires doctors to obtain patient consent to share data with third parties. Third parties include quality standards/registers. Under Wgbo, patients are required to provide explicit consent for their records to be included within the Landelijk Schakel Punt (LSP). As a result, the exchange is missing data on non-consenting patients and for patients whose health care provider did not ask them to provide consent. This limits the reliability of the data for direct care or secondary uses.

New framework law is a good start but will need follow-on administrative orders and policies to achieve the desired result

A new framework law (Wegiz) introduced in 2021 aiming to improve health data interoperability takes a cautious and incremental approach, raising concerns among experts interviewed that full health data interoperability would not be achieved. Experts interviewed indicate that the law asks health care professionals to set standards for treatment. The standards are then submitted to the National Quality Register, which has a legal status. When the National Quality Register adopts the standard, it would become a norm that the Inspectorate has the authority to uphold. The ministry would then 'translate' these professional standards into technical/informational requirements.

The framework law will likely require additional follow-on administrative orders to authorise the new standards called for by professional groups. Experts interviewed are concerned that the process could be slow and potentially result in conflicting and incomplete sets of standards. To avoid this, follow-on administrative orders could take a more holistic approach, broadening the conditions for agreed data standards for all the purposes in the public interest (direct care and secondary data uses that would benefit the public, including quality monitoring). Follow-on administrative orders must also ensure that standards are not limited to health care data, but also include public health and social care data which are key to an integrated health information system.

A recent letter from Minister De Jonge to parliament (15 October 2021) outlies ways in which implementation of the Wegiz is being expedited.

Further development and implementation of information standards (technical "how") and quality standards (clinical "what") is foreseen

The Framework law requires the development and implementation of information standards and complementary quality standards. Evaluating and adopting standards is a complex undertaking. Before recommending standards, it will be necessary to evaluate whether health care providers and organisations could conform to new requirements and the evaluation will necessitate acquiring knowledge about the various IT architectures and software in current use including the different structured terminology standards and uses of free text (unstructured data). Supporting health care providers and organisations to adopt standards will require implementation guidelines that are feasible and specific enough for IT developers to implement within diverse architectures, terminologies, data quality standards and other variations across the Dutch health information system landscape. Since quality registers may not have expertise in IT architectures, software development or existing IT systems, it will be essential to support quality registers with a consortium of partners with health informatics skills.

A useful reference for the scope of this work may be the HL7 Clinical Quality Information Work Group and the related Da Vinci Project (see Box 3.2). These projects of HL7 require a diverse set of partners with skills encompassing the full spectrum of the project, particularly experts in the IT architectures and software who can prepare implementation guidelines and draft software codes for IT developers to follow so that clinical information systems might be adapted to produce the desired data and information.

> **Box 3.2. HL7 Clinical Quality Information Work Group and Da Vinci Project**
>
> The Clinical Quality Information (CQI) Work Group is creating and maintain HL7 standards in support of measuring and reporting on quality in health care including dimensions of safety, effectiveness, patient centredness, timeliness, efficiency and equity. To do this, the Work Group collaborates with other HL7 Work Groups with expertise in data models, content, and expressions that can affect the measurement of quality of care. Communication is frequent with the following Work Groups: Clinical Information Modeling Initiative (CIMI), Fast Healthcare Interoperability Resources (FHIR), Implementable Technology Specifications (ITS), Patient Care (PC), Structured Documents (SD), Orders and Observations (O&O) and Pharmacy (Pharm).
>
> The HL7 Da Vinci project is working to solve data interoperability problems to enable value based care. Da Vinci is a private sector driven initiative of US health care payers, providers and IT software vendors that work together to define business problems, identify the corresponding data exchange requirements and use that information to draft standards in the form of implementation guides and sample software code.
>
> Outputs of the Work Group and Da Vinci include standards specifications and implementation guides that provide detailed guidance for IT developers to follow. Before such work is adopted, there is a process to review and test new specifications and there are levels of approval within HL7 that must be passed.
>
> Source: HL7 (n.d.[8]), "Clinical Quality Information", https://www.hl7.org/Special/committees/cqi/index.cfm; HL7 (n.d.[9]), "Da Vinci Project", https://confluence.hl7.org/display/DVP/Da+Vinci+Welcome.

A national Common Data Model would facilitate data exchange for many beneficial purposes

In the near term, the Netherlands could standardise health data to support health care quality measurement and information by mapping/re-coding data from the diverse array of information systems in the

Netherlands to a common data model (CDM). While this may not be feasible for health organisations with the most customised and irregular IT systems, it may be possible for most health care providers and organisations holding health data to have their existing data mapped/re-coded to a CDM.

Erasmus University MC leads the development of an open science federated network of data providers in Europe called the European Health Data & Evidence Network (EHDEN) that are coding health and health care data to the global Observational Medical Outcomes Partnership (OMOP) common data model (EHDEN, 2021[1]). There are six data partners in this project within the Netherlands who have coded their data to OMOP CDM including the Erasmus Integrated Primary Care Information (IPCI) database which is based on data from primary care electronic medical records. The IPCI data is from a Netherlands' network of over 600 General Practitioners whose electronic medical record systems involve a variety of different software vendors. Recently, the electronic medical records of Erasmus MC have also been coded to OMOP CDM so the hospital could participate in international COVID-19 research.

Other data coded to OMOP CDM include the National Intensive Care Evaluation (NICE) quality registry that is based on intensive care data extracted from electronic health records of hospitals, the Foundation for the Provision of Information for Care and Research (STIZON) which includes data on prescription medications data from pharmacy records and electronic patient records within hospitals and GPs; the Netherland's data of the European Society for Blood and Marrow Transplantation (EBMT) and the Netherlands Integral Cancer Centre (IKNL) and data from the electronic patient records of the University of Amsterdam MC. An expert interviewed for this study reported that the Health RI initiative in the Netherlands is exploring the use of the OMOP CDM to facilitate clinical data analysis.

Through EHDEN's funding, the coding of participating organisation's data to the OMOP CDM is financially supported up to 100K Euros per organisation. The cost of mapping data is particularly high among organisations whose data don't already conform to global clinical terminology standards, such as SNOMED-CT, so the funding requirements for mapping data to the OMOP CDM in the Netherlands could be significant.

Throughout Europe there are partners in the EHDEN federated network in 20 countries including public sector and private sector partners. EHDEN is funded by the European Union and EFPIA and is affiliated with the global OHDSI project and part of the same federated network. The OHDSI project and its OMOP CDM have been implemented in 74 countries and have over 2 700 collaborating partners. While used for a wide range of health and health care research, a recent example is the ability of this network to respond to the COVID-19 pandemic. There are over 200 COVID-19 research papers in Google Scholar that refer to the OMOP CDM, with dozens of citations for multi-country studies involving the Netherlands' EHDEN partners.

Participation in the OMOP CDM is growing within the OECD. To support COVID-19 research, the Korean Government recently funded coding the health insurance claims records for the full population which are held by HIRA (Health Insurance Review and Assessment Agency), as well as COVID-19 case data from the disease control agency (KCDA) and other data to the OMOP CDM for research undertaken through OHDSI regarding COVID-19 patient treatments and outcomes. The Korean Government is also funding hospitals to recode their data to OMOP CDM. In France, the Health Data Hub is working to code its data holdings on the population of France to the OMOP to support COVID-19 research. Other countries reporting to the OECD in 2021 that they were coding electronic clinical records to the OMOP common data model included Australia and Israel.

The Centraal Bureau voor de Statistiek (CBS) exemplifies good practice, but its remit is limited

Interviews with experts conducted as part of this review identified the CBS as a model for the appropriate implementation of GDPR requirements and a privacy-by-design approach to data development, linkage, sharing and accessibility that is secure and privacy-protective. Several health care data custodians indicated that they are sharing their data with the CBS and that they benefit from the CBS' secure remote data access facility when their data are shared with external researchers.

Experts from CBS have indicated that they welcome expanding their data holdings of health and health care data and have ambitious plans for providing secure data access within the ODISSEI initiative which includes advanced technical infrastructure and computing power for complex data analysis and software development. Indeed, experts report that CBS is becoming the main provider of secure remote data access services in the Netherlands for both health and social-economic data.

However, CBS experts also report that their authorising legislation makes it difficult for them to receive health datasets from other organisations because they are, by law, required to create national statistics from any dataset they accept. Under these arrangements, CBS cannot become a hub for secure health data linkage and access for research purposes.

Further, CBS is not funded to provide data linkage and access to data. It employs a cost-recovery model that experts interviewed indicate is expensive. The ODISSEI initiative, for example, has funding from universities through scientific grants that help to offset the costs of data access for research. Health-RI is funded through government grants (See below).

The approach to electronic health and medical records is un-co-ordinated

A well designed, longitudinal (interoperable) electronic health record (eHR) system can greatly enhance care quality – especially co-ordination and integration – as well as supply valuable information for research, innovation and public health. For example, an individual with multiple health problems can manage their health much better if they have access to their own medical information, and if all their health care providers – GPs, specialists, hospitals, emergency rooms, pharmacists, dieticians and physiotherapists – also have access to the same information. Patient Internet Portals to their own current medical records from multiple health care providers exist now in most OECD countries as discussed in Chapter 2.

Moreover, data can be extracted from the eHR system for quality monitoring, clinical registries and health statistics which is common practice among many OECD countries now. The data within the eHR system can be linked to other datasets to, for example, develop machine learning algorithms to predict the mortality risk in sub-strata of patients thereby improving the safety and effectiveness of care in close to real-time. Such risk stratification models are being developed in Israel and Spain.

A longitudinal eHR system does not mean a single, centralised electronic medical record (eMR). It can equally comprise a distributed network of eMRs belonging to hospitals, specialists' rooms, GPs and pharmacies if the technical and operational infrastructure exists for data to be standardised and exchanged between them, and where people can access all their own health information in one place. The lack of eMR interoperability means that patients and the public are missing out on better care and more knowledge to improve care co-ordination and integration, public health, and research and innovation.

The Netherlands is lagging other countries in eMR interoperability

The situation in the Netherlands is not as advanced as in many other OECD countries regarding interoperability of medical data as was discussed in Chapter 2. While notable initiatives such as MedMij and LSP are trying to address this, the lack of co-ordination and steering is evident.

Experts interviewed described that most health care organisations have engaged software vendors to develop bespoke eHR platforms to specifications that suit their requirements and priorities. In most cases, and in the absence of an overarching national data strategy and governance framework, little attention has been paid to exchanging data. Experts described that many providers are locked into agreements with their vendors, who either limit or charge large sums to retrofit interoperability and exchange capability into their systems.

Stakeholder interviews suggest that patients often need to bring paper records of their health information to different practitioners, and that general practitioners are unable to share important data such as COVID-19 vaccination status with public health officials. Recent media reports describe patients transferred between hospitals needing to carry a CD containing their medical information because the hospitals' eMRs cannot exchange data.[2]

Collaboration and data exchange are limited for other reasons

An integrated health information system means that all types of health care, public health and social care data can flow to where they are needed and are fit for use upon arrival. In the context of the Dutch health system, this means enabling secure data exchange across the numerous silos and requiring strict technical and semantic interoperability standards.

Timely and secure data exchange opens entirely new possibilities in biomedical science as well as health service design and delivery. For example, the capacity to link various clinical, administrative and social datasets to study the safety and effectiveness of COVID-19 vaccines in various population sub-groups in real time. Results can alert providers and policy makers to potential risks and opportunities, as well as contribute to global efforts to control the pandemic. Such studies have recently been conducted in Israel and Scotland.

In another example, New Zealand has been able to generate 'virtual' registries by harvesting data from a range of sources, saving time and resources. Virtual registries and statistical databases based on data extracted from EHR systems for national health monitoring were reported in 2021 in 12 countries (see Chapter 2).

Despite many stakeholders' best efforts over the past decade, experts interviewed described how strong collaboration and smooth exchange of data are largely lacking in the Netherlands. This can be attributed to several legal and policy barriers discussed in this section.

Rules to protect competition inhibit collaboration and data exchange

The managed competition model forms the basis of a large part of the Dutch health system. This requires, by definition, a strong regulatory framework. However, some regulations and policies are in direct opposition to promoting data integration. For example, to protect the functioning of the health care market, collaboration between providers is monitored by the Netherlands Authority for consumers and markets (acm.nl). Experts described that, under this authority, collaboration among health care providers is generally prohibited except under certain conditions.

The tension between supporting market competition and fostering smooth, secure data exchange and, more broadly, collaboration among providers, needs to be explicitly acknowledged and addressed.

Agreements lack requirements for data interoperability that cannot be overcome by voluntary data exchange initiatives

Experts interviewed explained that multiple institutes are funded by the government to collect data on aspects of health or parts of the health care system. However, funding is not contingent upon collaboration among them and data interoperability among them is not required.

Similarly, 'hoofdlijnakkoorden' (outline agreements) between the government and specific sectors such as medical specialists, include agreements on finances and quality but not on data interoperability. As a result, sectors continue to operate in silos.

Experts also explained that standards developed by either Nictiz or MedMij are voluntary and participation in a data exchange is voluntary.

Further, experts described that while the government provides financial incentives to physicians and hospitals to become MedMij certified; certification does not include verification that the data within MedMiJ are interoperable, nor verification that the user experience for patients would meet reasonable expectations. For example, verification of how well health information is integrated and presented to the patient is not included.

Data coverage gaps are evident

Two private data exchanges exist: LSP for exchange among providers and MedMij for exchange between providers and patients. Experts interviewed explained that the LSP is a centralised architecture and the MedMij is developed through open Application Programming Interfaces. A decision is needed to develop a harmonised approach, which would allow for exchange among all stakeholders and avoid unnecessary duplication. Both exchanges are non-binding and therefore they are incomplete, which limits their usefulness for direct care and secondary uses and compromises patient safety.

Experts explained that under current policy, MedMij is conditional upon a patient having a PGO (personal data environment). Patients without a PGO will be missing from MedMij. Also, patients who see providers that are not MedMij certified will be missing part of their health records. For health care providers, MedMij will be an incomplete information source, missing patients and providing incomplete information for patients.

Further, experts also indicated that Personal data environments (PGO) are evolving for sub-sets of patients rather than toward an integrated PGO that provides a complete source of information. The consequence will be that many patients may never have a complete picture of their health and health care within a single PGO. This problem will likely be most evident for patients with multi-morbidity or complex health and social care needs.

The Landelijk Schakel Punt (LSP) is funded by health insurers. Costs to participate are borne by health care providers and legislation requiring consent (see above) limits its usefulness because some patients are inevitably missing and there are missing data for included patients.

Costs of interoperability are high and exacerbated by information blocking

The Dutch Government plans to invest in integrated care through the 'right care at the right place' initiative. Integrated care requires data interoperability among health and social care providers. In addition to legal barriers to the exchange of data that were discussed earlier, there are resource and technical constraints to health data exchange that will limit reaching the goal of integrated care.

Experts interviewed explained that a large vendor of electronic health record system software in the Netherlands, which provides eHR software to both hospitals and primary care offices, has an IT architecture that limits data exchange and locks health care providers out of accessing their own data.

Experts interviewed indicate that hospitals and medical offices are unable to access their own data and must go through the software vendor to enable data exchange or to enable views of their data (business intelligence tools). This creates a financial disincentive for health care providers to exchange data, as they face financial charges to do so. Further, when financial incentives may be provided by the government to encourage data exchange, the rewards are taken up by the fees of the software provider.

Health care providers experiencing this information blocking are also limited in their ability to adopt new devices, apps and decision-support tools that are set up for a modern IT architecture. At the same time, the Dutch technology sector is limited from creating devices, apps and tools that could be sold in both domestic and international markets.

The situation is likely to continue without legislation, certification and financial incentives to prevent information blocking by software vendors and to encourage software vendors to provide modern IT architectures that support data exchange and analytical uses of data that are in the public interest. This can, in fact, create a level playing field for competition and the market to thrive while advancing public policy objectives.

An updated reimbursement model would create better incentives to collaborate

The current health care remuneration model encourages more activity and service volume. In addition to laws explicitly forbidding collaboration (see previous sections), funding based on fee-for-service further disincentivises collaboration and integration of care across sectors and settings because the provider is rewarded simply for their input item in the broader care cycle. Not only can this result in sub-optimal patient experiences and health outcomes, but it is also often more expensive.

Experts interviewed explained that there are calls to change the funding model to encourage co-ordination and value across entire cycles of care, as opposed to paying for processes and inputs. Bundled payments for an entire care pathway from initial diagnosis to an agreed endpoint can potentially address this problem. Several initiatives using bundled payments have emerged in the Netherlands over the past few years, but this model is not yet the norm.

Because care integration also relies on sharing information about patients and processes, financially rewarding joined-up care and outcomes will de facto also encourage the sharing of information about patients' health and their care. Funding reforms are therefore an integral part of creating an environment where data linkage and exchange makes financial sense. The business case will strengthen if collaboration is rewarded.

Experts interviewed also raised concern about incentives. In the absence of financial incentives for data interoperability, the benefits of data interoperability and integration mainly accrue to government, researchers and health insurers; while the costs of improving the interoperability of health information systems are mainly borne by health care providers. Government leadership and legislative and policy tools are needed to create the right environment for information exchange and collaboration.

The Netherlands risks being left behind on research and innovation

Many countries are gearing up to use data, including health data, as the fuel to power research and innovation. The Netherlands risks being left behind in this regard unless current deficiencies in data governance, interoperability and exchange are addressed. A recent Open Data Institute report put the Netherlands in the 'limited vision' category for advancing the secondary use of health data when compared with other EU countries (Boyd M, 2021[10]).

There are worrying signs. As a result of the various issues with data access and interoperability outlined in the previous sections, interview subjects reported that researchers and AI developers in the Netherlands are frequently working with patient clinical data from other countries, such as the United States and China. Emerging EU requirements for a Health Data Space (see Chapter 2) should be seen as an opportunity to capitalise on secure use of health data for secondary purposes.

Dutch initiatives – Health-RI & ODISSEI – and EU EHDEN exhibit the right approach

While there are many health data custodians in the Netherlands, three research infrastructures have emerged whose aims and purpose align with those envisaged for Health Data Spaces.

Hospitals in the Netherlands have provided start-up funding to create the Health Research Infrastructure initiative (Health-RI) which aims to "establish an interconnected data infrastructure for Dutch personalised medicine and health research" (Dutch Tech Centre for Life Sciences, 2021[2]). Experts interviewed indicate that Health-RI would like to access data within hospital and GP electronic health record systems for approved research projects in real time.

Health-RI intends to use the personal health train concept to protect privacy and data security. With the personal health train, analytics and other software code (research questions) travel *to* the data only research results (answers) flow back to the researcher. This the Netherlands innovation is a new privacy-enhancing technology that embodies 'privacy-by-design'. Health-RI recently received a funding boost of EUR 69 million from the Dutch Government National Growth Fund (Health-RI, 2021[11]). Ongoing funding for the initiative may be considered to cement its role in the Dutch health data ecosystem.

ODISSEI (Open Data Infrastructure for Social Science and Economic Innovations) provides researchers with access to the data holdings of the CBS, including the micro-data in-flowing to CBS from Dutch Hospitals, GPs, health insurers and research institutes as well as health survey data and information on the health care industry (ODISSEI, 2021[12]).

Experts interviewed explained that ODISSEI follows 'privacy-by-design' practices to offer secure data linkage services and secure access to data, as well as an advanced computing and analytic capacity. Funding for ODISSEI is through scientific grants that subsidise the costs of data linkages, infrastructure and secure access to data enabling CBS to provide services to ODISSEI members at a lower cost.

ODISSEI's membership includes social data research centres and, more recently, medical research centres have joined as observers. Experts interviewed explained that medical research centres are attracted to the model ODISSEI provides, where ODISSEI sets the research strategy and the CBS provides data curation, linkage and secure remote data access. Further, there is interest in the research community to bring the social sciences and the life sciences closer together because of their overlapping research objectives and data needs.

Health research projects, particularly those in the public health domain where the influences of environment, health behaviours and socio-economic factors are important, take place within ODISSEI. For example, recent projects include a study examining genome-wide associations with health care costs and an analysis of how behaviours and inequalities spread through social networks. There are, however, important research centres and health data that are outside of ODISSEI. Experts interviewed explained, for example, that it has not been possible to link the social networking model developed within ODISSEI to the COVID-19 case data collected by the Rijksinstituut voor Volksgezondheid en Milieu (RIVM). If such exchanges were more feasible, then it would be possible to leverage the investment in the social networking model to predict how and where the pandemic may be spreading, and which population groups are at highest risk. This information could guide public policy decisions.

ODISSEI reports a shortfall in governmental funding for national cohort surveys that follow individuals over a long period of time. Longitudinal data from cohorts provides unique information about how the trajectory of individuals' health, behaviours and environments influence their future health outcomes and health care use. Such data is not available from clinical or administrative data sources.

As the strategy for an integrated health information system is developed, it will be important to consider how the Health RI project and the ODISSEI project can be connected with one another and with all the key data that are needed for the Netherlands to reach its public policy goals.

The Netherlands participation in the EU EHDEN project (introduced earlier and led by Erasmus MC) is a further exhibition of best practices. Through EHDEN, participating organisations re-code their health and clinical data to the OMOP Common Data Model. Participating organisations are part of a federated network with a privacy-by-design approach. The data within the network always remain in the custody of the organisations holding them and therefore remain under the legal and policy frameworks of the data holding organisations. Researchers can view the specifications for the common data model and may query the data using a tool provided (ATLAS) or may submit customised statistical or software code. Researchers cannot access or even visualise the underlying microdata held by the participating organisations and therefore privacy and data security risks are greatly reduced which is how EHDEN and the affiliated OHDSI project can develop multi-country health research in a timely way. A further accelerator of the timeliness of research within the EHDEN federated network is from the open science method of sharing code through GitHub, supporting interoperability of data analytics as well as of data. For example, standardised analytics codes in the R statistical language for commonly used statistical methods/applications are shared and individual researchers contribute and re-use codes.

As was discussed earlier, the OMOP CDM is a tool the Netherlands can use to overcome health data interoperability problems in the near term. This tool would work very well within the ODISSEI and Health RI projects, particularly to ensure that a personal health train approach could work in practice as it is already applied for distributed analytics within the EHDEN and OHDSI federated networks.

References

Boyd M, Z. (2021), *Secondary Use of Health Data in Europe*, Open Data Institute, http://theodi.org/wp-content/uploads/2021/09/Secondary-use-of-Health-Data-In-Europe-ODI-Roche-Report-2021-5.pdf. [10]

Dutch Tech Centre for Life Sciences (2021), *Health-RI*, https://www.dtls.nl/large-scale-research-infrastructures/health-ri/. [2]

EDPS (2020), *Preliminary Opinion 8/2020 on the European Health Data Space.*, https://edps.europa.eu/sites/default/files/publication/20-11-17_preliminary_opinion_health_data_space_en.pdf. [5]

EHDEN (2021), *European Health Data and Evidence Network*, https://www.ehden.eu/. [1]

Health-RI (2021), *Dutch Government has pledged 69 million euros investment to Health-RI*, https://www.health-ri.nl/news/dutch-government-has-pledged-69-million-euros-investment-health-ri. [11]

HL7 (n.d.), *Clinical Quality Information*, Health Level Seven International, https://www.hl7.org/Special/committees/cqi/index.cfm. [8]

HL7 (n.d.), *Da Vinci Project*, Health Level Seven International, https://confluence.hl7.org/display/DVP/Da+Vinci+Welcome. [9]

Loohuis, K. (2021), *Data of Thousands of Dutch Citizens Leaked from Government Covid-19 Systems*, https://www.computerweekly.com/news/252495983/Data-of-thousands-of-Dutch-citizens-leaked-from-government-Covid-19-systems. [4]

Oderkirk, J. (2021), "Survey results: National health data infrastructure and governance", *OECD Health Working Papers*, No. 127, OECD Publishing, Paris, https://doi.org/10.1787/55d24b5d-en. [3]

ODISSEI (2021), *Open Data Infrastructure for Social Science and Economic Innovations*, https://odissei-data.nl/en/. [12]

OECD (2020), "Opportunities and Challenges of Blockchain Technologies in Health Care", *OECD Blockchain Policy Series*, OECD, Paris, https://www.oecd.org/finance/Opportunities-and-Challenges-of-Blockchain-Technologies-in-Health-Care.pdf. [7]

Oliveira Hashiguchi, T., L. Slawomirski and J. Oderkirk (2021), "Laying the foundations for artificial intelligence in health", *OECD Health Working Papers*, No. 128, OECD Publishing, Paris, https://dx.doi.org/10.1787/3f62817d-en. [6]

Notes

1   https://eenvandaag.avrotros.nl/item/gegevens-op-de-fax-of-een-dvd-bij-verplaatsing-van-coronapatienten-wordt-gemis-van-elektronisch-patientendossier-wel-heel-duidelijk/.

2   https://eenvandaag.avrotros.nl/item/gegevens-op-de-fax-of-een-dvd-bij-verplaatsing-van-coronapatienten-wordt-gemis-van-elektronisch-patientendossier-wel-heel-duidelijk/.

4 Towards an integrated health information system in the Netherlands

This chapter describes the legal, policy and operational changes that are needed in the Netherlands to establish an integrated health information system. It sets out the requirements to take advantage of the strengths and to address the problems uncovered in this review of the current Dutch health information system. The recommendations include an overarching requirement to approach health data more as a public good than as a commodity, and to develop and implement a national digital health strategy that strengthens mutual trust across all stakeholder groups. A range of policy actions to implement the national digital health strategy are recommended in this chapter, including the need for technical infrastructure and interoperability standards, and an overarching data governance framework that includes greater harmonisation of policies and practices to ensure privacy and promote data security.

Many OECD countries have started harnessing their health data to work to achieve their public policy objectives. Although the health systems are all organised and funded differently, they share some common features: an integrated health information system based on a co-ordinated strategy that is supported by strong leadership and a specifically designed data governance framework.

The preceding two chapters described how personal health data, as well as other data relevant to health and well-being, are managed, exchanged, and deployed to advance policy objectives in the Netherlands including service improvement, better public health, research outputs and innovation. Despite some considerable strengths and advantages, the current health information landscape is too fragmented to achieve these goals and presents a risk to the Netherlands of falling behind other countries in a range of social and economic domains.

This chapter outlines legal, policy and operational changes to establish an integrated health information system. It sets out the requirements to take advantage of strengths described in the previous chapter and to address the problems uncovered in this study.

The first requirement is a mindset that sees data as a public good and a resource that can be harnessed to advance the health and welfare of the Dutch people. This needs to be embodied in a National Strategy that must be developed inclusively and be trusted by all stakeholders. A range of policies, regulations and enabling legislation will be needed to implement the national strategy. Technical infrastructure and standards will need to be implemented. An overarching governance framework will be required, including greater harmonisation of data privacy and security policies and practices.

Steps toward an integrated HIS

The foundation of a modern, 21st century health information system that seeks to embrace the opportunities of health data while protecting individuals' rights to privacy is a modern, robust data governance framework. Such a framework comprises legislation, policy and regulation on standardisation, interoperability, and exchange; on security and privacy requirements; and on public transparency and engagement to ensure necessary levels of trust among the public and other key stakeholders. In effect, it is a technical, policy and political apparatus.

A cohesive, national framework is necessary in any context, but especially in countries with a fragmented health data ecosystem such as the Netherlands. The alternative – a collection of data silos that cannot and/or will not exchange valuable information, and where management of data security and privacy risks is ad hoc and very variable – is not in the interest of patients, providers, industry, governments, or the public, and will hinder the realisation of the four policy goals outlined in the introduction.

Radical health system reform is not needed

The Dutch health system has served the country very well in the 20th century. But the challenges and opportunities of the 21st century are vastly different, and the increasing quantity of generated health data calls for a political choice, legislative guidance and fitting strategic action in order to facilitate ethical and optimal use of this rapidly expanding commodity. The challenge does not lie within specific actors in the health system, but across all of them. There is a need to have a common infrastructure in order to have health data that is fit for use and purpose for each actor's mandate in the health system because, fundamentally, most health system actors are reliant on data generated by others to achieve their objectives.

Building the tracks and the signals, to create an integrated health information system that meets the needs and opportunities of the 21st century will require a unified national strategy (preferably aligned with a broader national digital/data strategy). It will require a new set of institutional function to develop, implement and oversee a health data infrastructure and integrated information system, either through a new national authority or by consolidating and strengthening the remit, function, and competencies of existing agencies. Successful implementation will require good governance, policy, and trust among all stakeholders.

A unified, national strategy is needed

A **strategic plan** is a common first step toward an integrated health information system. Developing a strategy should consider the data assets and information infrastructure already in place and build forward from them to develop the tracks and signals that are missing. Key to the development of the strategy will be working with stakeholders to determine the objectives of the strategy and the values that the stakeholders want to uphold.

It is essential that the strategy is sufficiently **broad and deep**. Breadth refers to incorporating the four main data types: health care, public health, social care and long-term care data. Depth ensures that all data are included, and that they can be linked at the individual level to enable better care integration as well as more precision and scope in secondary uses.

An important accompaniment to the digital strategy are roadmaps for each strategic objective, particularly those that will be challenging to achieve, such as data interoperability. The roadmaps should be specific about who is responsible for what and when deliverables can be expected. The roadmaps should address the full breadth and depth of the strategy to ensure a balanced and coherent strengthening of the Dutch health information system. Hence not only enhancement of interoperability and secondary use of data in clinical care but inclusion of data uses in public health, long term care and social care.

Figure 4.1 presents a graphical overview of the recently published national digital strategy of New Zealand, which includes many goal posts that would resonate in the Netherlands such as: digital services and health information contribute to patient empowerment; health care quality and outcomes are improved; health system performance is strengthened; and there is greater capacity for evidence-based decision-making.

Essential elements include those that enable the strategy to be realised at a policy level, such as legal reforms, policy guidelines, governing and operational bodies, and financial incentives; as well as those that enable the strategy at a technical level, such as data architecture, technical infrastructure and terminology and interoperability standards.

Figure 4.1. New Zealand Digital Health Strategic Framework

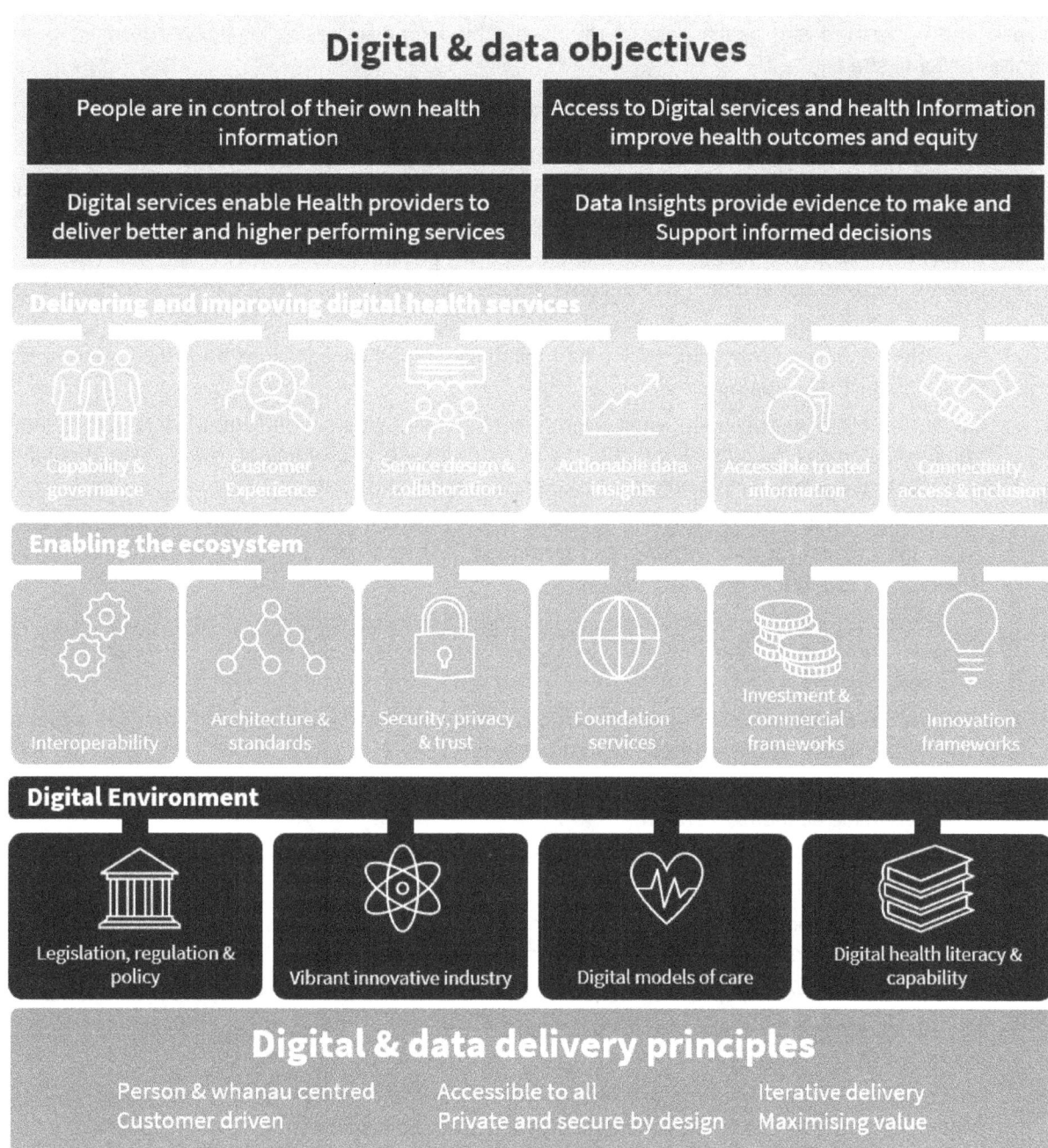

Source: Ministry of Health, New Zealand (2020[1]), "Digital Health Strategic Framework", https://www.health.govt.nz/our-work/digital-health/digital-health-strategic-framework.

A national strategy will require leadership and expertise

The Ministerie van Volksgezondheid, Welzijn en Sport (VWS) would take the lead in the development of the national strategy. Indeed, all experts interviewed for this country review called for leadership from the ministry to build the tracks and the signals. The ministry must be supported in developing the strategy by experts, particularly external experts in health data informatics, data interoperability and health data science, as well as external experts in 'privacy-by-design' approaches to health data governance.

Internal support will also be needed for the ministry to build a team to take the lead. The ministry could consider creating a new unit and engaging or seconding experts in health information systems, health data science and informatics and health data governance. This expertise will be essential to ensuring an effective national strategy.

The MHWS should lead the development of a national strategy. In doing so, the MHWS should:

1. **Build trust and support for the strategy among stakeholders and the public.**
   - Consult with governmental agencies (Informatie Beraad, IGJ, ZIN, NZa) on needs for information, analytics and information products.
   - Consult with non-government stakeholders especially patient groups, regions and municipalities, provider organisations, health professional groups, insurers, academia, biomedical industry and software vendors.
   - Develop and implement a public information campaign, public consultations and other avenues for public input into the strategy.
   - Conduct public consultations at all stages of development of the national health data governance framework and provide public information, such as a website, to disseminate information about the development process and its outcome, as part of the National Strategy.
   - Launch a government campaign with communication experts to promote a dialogue with the public about the benefits of data sharing and exchange, with the goal of valuing health data in the Netherlands as a public good (see below).
     - This public dialogue must assuage public and stakeholder concerns about privacy risks and reassure them by clearly communicating about how privacy will be protected when data are used.

2. **Draft the high-level IT architecture/infrastructure for an integrated health information system that meets the information needs of key stakeholders.**
   - Review existing architectures within and outside of the Netherlands and improved architectures proposed in the academic literature.
   - Review existing data exchanges to co-ordinate, integrate and ensure the exchange meets the needs of all stakeholders.
   - Review and recommend global standards for data exchange and semantic interoperability, taking into consideration developments and requirements within the EU.
   - Include privacy-by-design protections, particularly federated learning (distributed analytics).
   - Include interoperability in analytics, information and knowledge and foster the adoption of a global common data model (CDM).
   - Include lifecycle interoperability to ensure analytical uses of historical data as the information system evolves (i.e. ensure health trajectories and longitudinal data analysis are supported).

3. **Further develop and strengthen the national health data governance legislative framework to support the national strategy. The framework must align with European regulations and should specify the following.**
   - The requirements for uniform data standards for health terminology, data exchange, interoperability and a common health data model.
   - The requirements for the exchange, access to and use of data to serve the health-related public interest.
   - The requirements for data security and privacy protection by design ('privacy-by-design').

4. **Lead the legislative and policy reforms necessary to realise the strategy, in consultation with other areas of government where needed.**
   - Draft the role and mandate of the national authority responsible for the implementation, maintenance, and oversight of the integrated health information system (see next section for detailed functions of such an authority).
   - Develop policy tools and financial incentives to realise the strategy.

5. **Develop the draft roadmaps for each strategic objective within the national strategy.**
   - Ensure that the roadmaps are specific regarding who is responsible for each step and when results can be expected.

Role of the MHWS in the implementation of the integrated health information system:

- Ensure the MHWS oversees the national agency and is engaged in strategic planning and strategic decision-making (see the next section regarding the role of the national agency).
- Evaluate and publicly report on progress in the implementation of the national strategy.
- Facilitate progress in policy and legal reforms to support the on-going development of the integrated health information system in consultation with the national agency and the Informatieberaad Zorg.
- Develop and maintain analytics products and dashboards for ministerial policy making and reporting.
- Co-ordinate planning and funding of health information projects within the ministry to align them with the strategy.
- Develop campaigns and tools to improve public transparency about health information, information governance and public benefits from improvements in health information.
- Review planning and funding of health information projects within the ministry to ensure they align with and contribute to the strategy and do not detract from or create disincentives to advance the strategy.

Key competencies to develop and implement the strategy:

- Strategic planning of health information projects,
- Evidence-based indicator development and policy analysis,
- Informatics (IT architecture, data exchange standards, semantic interoperability),
- Health data science (statistical and software development competencies, interoperability of analytics),
- Legislative frameworks,
- Privacy-by-design (privacy protection, data security and related information technology competencies), and
- Public consultation and communications/public relations.

Aligning with a broader national digital strategy

Considering the general nature of developing the strategy for an integrated health information system, incorporating it into a broader national strategy will be an advantage. In fact, most countries that are successfully digitalising their health systems have a national digital strategy – and data governance – that encompasses all areas of public policy including health. Estonia, for example, decided over two decades ago to become a 'digital society' meaning that 99% of public services, including health care are accessible virtually.[1] This has paid not only immense dividends during the COVID-19 pandemic, enabling the country's health, education and welfare systems to continue to function as normal, it has also promoted technological and policy advances in privacy and digital identity, made Estonia into Europe's top entrepreneurial hotspot according the World Economic Forum.[2]

Several Dutch experts and stakeholders interviewed emphasised their preference for need for a general national digital or data strategy. Some mentioned the approach taken in the field of education (i.e. SURF). Others mentioned initiatives of Municipalities and the Ministry of Internal Affairs which include social care data. In addition to the obvious synergies, the advantages of a cross-sector approach are particularly strong in the health arena given the value placed on privacy and security, the key role of non-health data (which can greatly enhance knowledge-generation), and the fact that makes a country more attractive for investment of biotech capital.

Institutional functions to develop, implement and oversee an integrated health information system

Implementing the National Strategy and operationalising its various facets can be described as 'building the tracks' of the integrated health information system. It will principally concern developing and maintaining consistent national data standards, and then certifying and incentivising actors to implement the strategy, including health care providers, software vendors and other developers of IT solutions. This will require a range of functions and competencies that are currently absent, without legal mandate or dispersed across various agencies in the Dutch health data landscape. These functions can be assigned to existing key institutions or be taken on by a new agency.

A national agency to implement and oversee the health information system

A single agency will be needed to co-develop and implement the national strategy and oversee/maintain the resulting health information system. This could be done by 'strengthening' or combining expertise of existing organisations or creating a new agency. In either case, this agency will have the authority to develop consistent national standards for semantics (terminology), electronic messaging (exchange), and data accessibility/sharing. It would also be responsible for keeping the standards up to date. Consider the roles of similar national agencies in Portugal and Estonia from Chapter 2. The national agency should also develop the national platform for public data exchange, acting as a hub through which the data flows to support secure access to and use of health data to serve the public interest. Consider the role of the French Health Data Hub, the Finnish FinData, the Australian DataPlace and the EU Health Data Space discussed in Chapter 2.

Many OECD countries have separate organisations responsible for national health data and for national electronic health record systems (see Chapter 2). This legacy has been problematic wherever there were no formal structures requiring the separate organisations to work closely together toward a common goal of enabling the secure primary and secondary use of health data. Working closely together is difficult because, for example, when tackling similar tasks, health statisticians and researchers within health data organisations differ from health informatics experts in both working methods and even in the vocabulary used to discuss the task. Further, the working methods and vocabularies of experts in health data privacy and security are more closely aligned with the legal community and are different from both health informatics and health statistics and research professionals. An integrated health information system is therefore dependent upon the effective integration of functions and of different professional groups who bring critical skills together to fulfil these functions.

The agency would best operate under a formal shared governance of standard setting with the existing health research infrastructure organisations and health information organisations (such as Health RI, CBS, ZiN, and ODDISEI), so that the standards developed will cover all data and data uses that are planned for within the National Strategy. It would have formal links with the IC as an advisory body for development and maintenance of technical standards.

The role of this authority would be responsible for standardisation, certification, a national public data platform and stakeholder consultation and engagement.

1. **Standardisation: Agreeing (or developing) and maintaining consistent national standards and keeping standards for:**
   - Semantics (terminology),
   - Electronic messaging (exchange),
   - Analytics (common data model, code sharing/analytics pipeline),
   - Data accessibility/sharing (prevent information blocking, secure (privacy-protective) data access, patient portals, health data space), and
   - Harmonisation of data privacy and security policies and practices including national guidance for health data processors.

2. **Certification and verification of compliance with national standards**
   - Certifying vendors of IT solutions and digital tools for compliance with national standards.
   - Certifying and verifying health care providers and other information system actors have achieved interoperability standards and are exchanging useable (quality) data and are not blocking data. This process must go beyond simply demonstrating that standards are used. Proof of data interoperability (exchange, data quality) should also be required to achieve certification.

3. **Building and maintaining a national public data platform for data exchange, acting as a hub through which the data flows to:**
   - Enable effective and secure processing of personal health data including data integration/linkage,
   - Foster adoption of a common health data model (CDM),
   - Manage the approval process for data integration and access requests involving data from multiple organisations,
   - Enable effective and secure mechanisms for access to personal health data for approved purposes, such as approved research,
   - Improve data quality, including conducing data quality auditing, and
   - Reduce overlapping and duplicative administrative and data processing activities among key stakeholders within the health information system.

4. **Stakeholder engagement and consultation to develop engagement in and support of the implementation of the national strategy through:**
   - Stakeholder and Public consultation about the national strategy and its implementation, and
   - Public transparency about the national strategy and the development, exchange, uses and data privacy and security protections of health data.

Governance of the national agency

The governance of the national agency requires consideration of the role such governance will play in effecting a change in the culture toward co-operation in health data development and exchange and in valuing health data as a public good.

To increase the buy-in and support for the agency and its mandate to implement the national strategy, it will be important to ensure that the national agency seeks the advice of and listens closely to the needs of all relevant stakeholder groups, such as the groups represented within the Informatieberaad Zorg today and health data infrastructure organisations, holders of key national health data, and health and medical research institutes and businesses who contribute to and depend upon the health information system, such representatives of pharmaceutical, medical device, data analytics, data applications and EHR system businesses. A potential advisory body is an expanded Health which is discussed further below.

The formal governance of the national agency must be appropriate to the Dutch context and culture. Consider, however, how frequently stakeholders will be engaged in advising the agency and the effort they will expend to do so and ensure that these organisations will realise a win-win from their participation.

Key competencies of the national agency:

- Strategic planning and management of health information projects,
- Evidence-based indicator development and policy analysis,
- Informatics (IT architecture, data exchange standards, semantic interoperability),
- Data science/analytics (statistical analysis, database architecture, coding, machine learning, distributed analytics, common data models, open science/code sharing),
- Systems testing, data quality checks and software evaluation including certification,
- Web and mobile applications development (websites, web portals and smartphone apps),
- Privacy by design (privacy protection, data security and related information technology competencies), and
- Public consultation and communications/public relations.

Technical infrastructure and standards

A key role of the new agency will relate to the technical infrastructure needed for an integrated health information system. Several requirements will also require attention, particularly if the system is to be retrofitted to the existing health system.

To facilitate information development and analytics, it will be necessary in many cases to re-code existing data to a common a data model (CDM). Leading global health data models, such as the OMOP (Observational Medical Outcomes Partnership) CDM, should be selected for this purpose and the technical capacity instituted.

Similarly, modern IT architecture and global standards for data terminology and exchange (messaging) should be deployed. For the Netherlands to participate in multi-country research and monitoring, the standards must comply with current and emerging European regulations. It will also be an advantage if the Netherlands participates in global and European efforts to develop global standards for health data terminology and exchange.

These functions can be performed by the agency responsible for operationalising the national strategy, in close liaison with the IC and Ministry. However, the need for expertise in IT architecture, informatics and data science is again emphasised.

The Informatieberaad Zorg as an advisory body to the national agency

A potential advisory body for developing and implementing the national strategy is already in place, the Informatieberaad Zorg. This body currently lacks a formal mandate and is missing participation from key organisations with responsibility for national health information and who contribute to and depend upon the health information system. Furthermore, its focus is presently on primary use of clinical data hence the needed broadening (to other sectors like public health, long term care and social care) and secondary data use needs to be reflected in either the composition of the IC or another mechanism of representation of stakeholders to assure an integrated health information system for the health system as a whole. Ensuring the IC includes representatives from key stakeholders in all aspects of an integrated health information system is highly recommended to make the most informed decisions about the strategy.

The Informatieberaad Zorg could become a forum of reflection and advice to the government and to the national agency. Specifically, its role would principally concern:

- Advising on the development and implementation of the national strategy for an integrated health information system, and
- Acting as ambassadors and spokespersons for the national strategy.

Membership of the Informatieberaad Zorg

Representatives within all key stakeholders in an integrated health information system, including organisations participating in the existing IC and new members representing organisations with responsibility for national health information (including health care, public health, social care and long-term care data); national health care quality registries; national health research infrastructures; organisations providing national health data access, linkage and governance; and businesses who contribute to and depend upon the health information system, such representatives of pharmaceutical, medical device, data analytics, data applications and EHR system businesses.

Members of the Informatieberaad Zorg should have executive or decision-making power within their respective organisations to provide strategic advice to the national agency on matters that may impact upon their organisations.

Implementation will hinge on governance, policy as well as trust

Key governance and policy reforms constitute 'the signals' that enable data to flow along the newly built tracks. These reforms will be executed by the ministry, with advice of the IC and the implementation capability of the national agency, and will primarily comprise developing new legislation, guidelines, governance, and funding mechanisms.

A legislative framework

Legal authority will be needed to authorise and finance the National Strategy and its implementation. This can be follow-on administrative orders to the new framework legislation for data exchange via care quality standards. They will complement the framework legislation and ensure depth and breadth (i.e. incorporate public health data and social care data and facilitate use of data for secondary purposes). The new administrative orders should require compliance with standards that ensure data interoperability and prevent data blocking by data custodians and software vendors.

Revisions may be needed to legacy legislations that are posing unnecessary obstacles to an integrated health information system, such as revisions to the *Medical Treatment Contracts Act (Wgbo)* to allow for lawful alternatives to consent for data exchange and uses in the public interest; to legislation authorising the Central Bureau of Statistics to allow it to act as a central hub for access to health datasets; and to regulations related to consumers and markets that prevent health care collaborations and data integration.

Building trust

The national strategy will steer the Netherlands away from the current situation of data silos toward an integrated system where secure data exchange is the norm. The strategy should modernise data development, exchange, management, and governance and it will require a change management approach that builds trust (See Box 4.1).

Box 4.1. Building Trust

Building trust among stakeholders and the public is an important aspect of health data governance and an effective data infrastructure. A lack of trust will undermine efforts to exchange data for primary and secondary purposes. First and foremost, trust is achieved through actions not words. Rhetoric must be matched by visible acts and changes to the status quo. It is a challenging process. While trust is established over a long time (years not months), it can be lost very quickly.

Any campaign to establish trust (and it should be approached as a campaign) should be based on transparency and inclusion. All stakeholders need to be part of developing and designing the change – in this case the strategy – from the beginning. Consultation on the finished product, developed by experts, will not achieve this. An iterative consultation process on the national strategy comprising 2 to 3 steps may take longer but will ensure people trust the finished product because inter alia they will have a sense of ownership and are invested in its success.

Transparency is key for establishing trust and for maintaining it. Key decisions, challenges, problems and resolutions should be communicated, and lines of accountability made clear. Successful countries have created public websites where people can access information about the strategy and everything concerning health data, its use, how it is managed and secured, how privacy is protected as well as the outputs of various programmes and projects that use personal health data.

Using health data to serve the public interest should be framed as an opportunity, not a risk. The long list of benefits should be explained in detail, using real-world examples. Every stakeholder group should be made aware how the changes will benefit them. For example: patients stand to receive modern health services, higher quality care and access to better, safe treatments; providers will have better data and information to improve practice and deliver high quality care; public health officials will have timely and complete information about infectious disease outbreaks, real-time data on vaccine safety and effectiveness, granular data to guide policies for managing NCDs; payers stand to access more detailed information on health care activity, costs and outcomes; policy makers will be better able to assess how the system performs and regulate it more intelligently; industry will have a tremendous resource to spur invention and technology; and society will benefit from an innovative and agile health sector that not only delivers the best possible outcomes but attracts investment and contributes to economic growth.

This way, the conversation can shift to a more complete view where NOT using data is a risk health and prosperity, and the discussion becomes how this can be done safely and securely. It is therefore crucial to be upfront about privacy, how it is secured, and how problems or failures are resolved. In fact, transparency is critically important when things don't go to plan. Nothing destroys trust faster than bad news being hidden. Equally, timely and clear communication about how past problems have been resolved can have a reassuring effect.

Finally, public education and PR campaigns need to be intelligently planned and rolled out. Engagement of professional expertise from advertising and communications are advised. Prominent 'champions' and thought-leaders from various walks of life should be co-opted to be part of the campaign promote the strategy. Alongside health and data science experts, it can be helpful to employ public figures (actors, musicians, footballers) to communicate the message. Getting the PR campaign wrong can have consequences. In 2014, the United Kingdom mailed out paper pamphlets to inform the public about health data governance under the care.data project. The campaign failed to get the public's attention and when public concerns about care.data arose later on they included the reaction that public consultation and communication about care.data were inadequate.

Source: OECD (2015[2]), *Health Data Governance: Privacy, Monitoring and Research*, https://dx.doi.org/10.1787/9789264244566-en.

The key will be to allocate sufficient time and resources to consultation with stakeholder bodies and the public at all points in the development of the strategy, so that progress from a draft strategy to a final strategy to roadmaps and implementation will feel natural, expected and safe.

Another key will be to have the right input in terms of technical, IT, policy, and legal expertise to develop a worthwhile and trustworthy strategy. Stakeholders will then be more at ease and comfortable to share their needs, their constraints, and their hopes for the strategy.

Members of the advisory body to the strategy, as well as the core strategy team, will be ambassadors and spokespersons for the strategy and should be encouraged to discuss the strategy widely with their communities and with the media to reach the public. For example, we understand from experts we interviewed that having leading Dutch experts speak to the media about the trustworthiness of the COVID-19 monitoring app alleviated the public's concerns about data privacy. The process of developing the strategy and roadmaps will result in a more complete and well-considered plan than can be developed through this OECD country review.

A firm hand will be needed to address resistance

From the outset it must be foreshadowed that an integrated health information system – as envisaged here – will be opposed and resisted by stakeholders who benefit from the current arrangements. For example, a firm hand will be needed with EHR system software vendors whose business model and products are out of alignment with global standards for clinical terminology and data exchange, and who do not support data interoperability within or across health care organisations.

These stakeholders may pressure the government to favour their local IT solutions, but unless compliant with international terminologies and electronic messaging standards, these solutions will not help the Dutch health technology sector to compete globally; will not allow local health care providers to adopt solutions/tools from the global marketplace; and will make progress toward the national strategy expensive, slow and probably impossible.

Regulation and guidelines

National policies will be needed to fulfil regulatory requirements that enable access to data for those who need them, while also keeping data secure and maintaining individuals' rights to privacy. These will guide:

- Implementing one national interpretation of the GDPR by all actors in the health information system,
- Emphasising privacy-by-design,
- Adhering to FAIR principles, and
- Developing reasonable approaches or lawful alternatives to consent.

It is critical that these national policies align with existing and developing guidance and regulations at the European level.

As part of this reform, the functionality and capacity of the two data exchanges (LSP and MedMij) should be harmonised to meet the needs of all stakeholders, including those currently using MedMij and LSP, and to realise the goals of the national strategy. The exchange of data should ensure full coverage of patients and providers and that patient records are complete. The exchange should be legally authorised, follow a 'privacy-by-design' approach and meet international standards for data security.

Complementary funding and incentives

To complement laws and policies, financial incentives will be needed to encourage compliance with national GDPR guidelines, with national data standards, and for demonstrating (verifiable) data interoperability.

This will require a review of government funding and subsidies of activities related to the exchange and use of health data, including research projects funded by government grants. It may also require explicit financial incentives to encourage health care providers and other actors to move to certified IT solutions and succeed in achieving verifiable interoperability.

The ministry and IC should consider how broader reforms to health care funding and remuneration that reward care co-ordination and value will affect the functioning of an integrated health information system.

References

Ministry of Health, New Zealand (2020), *Digital Health Strategic Framework*, https://www.health.govt.nz/our-work/digital-health/digital-health-strategic-framework. [1]

OECD (2015), *Health Data Governance: Privacy, Monitoring and Research*, OECD Health Policy Studies, OECD Publishing, Paris, https://dx.doi.org/10.1787/9789264244566-en. [2]

Notes

1 https://e-estonia.com/.

2 https://www.weforum.org/agenda/2020/07/estonia-advanced-digital-society-here-s-how-that-helped-it-during-covid-19/.

Annex A. Consultation with experts

The recommendations presented in this report were supported by a series of interviews and focus group discussions conducted by the OECD team with experts in the Netherlands from February to April 2021. Initial interview subjects were identified by the Ministry of Health and Welfare. These interview subjects recommended other experts for the OECD to consult. The OECD continued interviews until the information gathered from key informants began to share similar messages. Further rounds of interviews and focus groups took place from June to October 2021, gathering experts' reflections on proposed recommendations and expanding our understanding of the data landscape and recent innovations in the Netherlands.

The OECD thanks and appreciates the contributions of the following experts whose insights, experiences and aspirations informed the development of these recommendations.

Table A A.1. Experts interviewed about the health information system in the Netherlands

Name	Position	Organisation
Caroline A. Baan	Science Officer	Ministry of Health, Welfare and Sport
Frank Berens	Policy Advisor	V&VN
Adriaan Blankenstein	Chief Executive Officer	VZVZ (Association of care providers for care communication)
Hidde Boonstra		VNG
Teresa Cardosa	Senior Policy Advisor	ZiN Zorginstituut Nederland
Herko Coomans	Digital Health Policy Co-ordinator	Ministry of Health, Welfare and Sport
Dirk Deelstra	Senior Policy Advisor	ZiN Zorginstituut Nederland
Tom Emery	Deputy Director	Open Data Infrastructure for Social Science and Economic Innovations (ODISSEI)
Leone Flikweert	Chief Executive Officer	Health Research Infrastructure (Health RI)
Emi van Galen	Adviser	NZa
Jeroen Geelhoed	Senior Manager	BeBright Consulting
Ronald Gijsen	Researcher	Rijksinstituut voor Volksgezondheid en Milieu (RIVM)
Ivo LWJ Gorissen	Account Manager	Central Bureau of Statistics (CBS)
Jan Hazelzet	Professor in Healthcare Quality and Outcomes	Erasmus University Medical Centre
Marcel Heldoorn	Manager, Digital Healthcare	Netherlands Patient Federation
Peter Jansen	Information Manager	ZN (Organisation of health insurers)
Anil Jadoenathmisier	Director, IT and Innovation	Vereniging van Zorgaanbieders voor Zorgcommunicatie VZVZ
Sander Klous	Partner, Big Data Analytics	KPMG
Johan van Manen	Adviser	NZa
Frits van Merode	Researcher, Fac. Health, Medicine and Life Sciences	Maastricht University
Misja Mikkers	Chief Economist	NZa
Lokke Moerel	Professor of Global ICT Law	Tilburg University
Isabel Moll	Partner, Digital Trust Data (Healthcare)	KPMG
Annemiek Mulder	Senior Policy Advisor	ACTIZ (Organisation of LTC/home care providers)
Yola Park	Adviser, Information Policy	Ministry of Health, Welfare and Sport
Ron Rozendaal	Director, Information Policy and CIO	Ministry of Health, Welfare and Sport
Charlotte de Schepper	Representative	KNOV (Organisation of midwives)

Name	Position	Organisation
Gert-Jan van Boven	Chief Executive Officer	Dutch Hospital Data
Lies van Gennip	Director	Stichting PALGA (Pathology Registry)
J.A.M. van Oers (Hans)	Professor of Public Health	Tilburg University
Vincent Van Polanen Petel	Head, Health and Social Care Statistics	Central Bureau of Statistics (CBS)
Peter Rjinbeek	Deputy Head, Department of Medical Informatics and EU EHDEN Co-ordinator	Erasmus MC
Maarten van Rixtel	Chief Executive Officer	Sensor (Organisation of LTC/home care providers)
Tino de Velde		VNG
Inez Young	Chief Data Officer	Rijksinstituut voor Volksgezondheid en Milieu (RIVM)

Annex B. OECD Recommendation on Health Data Governance

The work of the OECD to support strengthening health data infrastructure and governance and to protect privacy and data security culminated in the OECD Recommendation on Health Data Governance [OECD/LEGAL/0433], which provides guidance for building national governance frameworks that enable personal health data to be both protected and used towards public policy goals.

The Recommendation applies to the access to, and the processing of, personal health data for health-related public interest purposes, such as improving health care quality, safety and responsiveness; reducing public health risks; discovering and evaluating new diagnostic tools and treatments to improve health outcomes; managing health care resources efficiently; contributing to the progress of science and medicine; improving public policy planning and evaluation; and improving patients' participation in and experiences of health care.

The Recommendation recommends that Adherents establish and implement a national health data governance framework to encourage the availability and use of personal health data to serve health-related public interest purposes while promoting the protection of privacy, personal health data and data security.

National health data governance frameworks should provide for:

- Engagement and participation of stakeholders in the development of a national health data governance framework;
- Co-ordination within government and co-operation among organisations processing personal health data to encourage common data-related policies and standards;
- Reviews of the capacity of public sector health data systems to serve and protect public interests;
- Clear provision of information to individuals about the processing of their personal health data including notification of any significant data breach or misuse;
- The processing of personal health data by informed consent and appropriate alternatives;
- The implementation of review and approval procedures to process personal health data for research and other health-related public interest purposes;
- Transparency through public information about the purposes for processing of personal health data and approval criteria;
- Maximising the development and use of technology for data processing and data protection;
- Mechanisms to monitor and evaluate the impact of the national health data governance framework, including health data availability, policies and practices to manage privacy, protection of personal health data and digital security risks;
- Training and skills development of personal health data processors;
- Implementation of controls and safeguards within organisations processing personal health data including technological, physical and organisational measures designed to protect privacy and digital security; and
- Requiring that organisations processing personal health data demonstrate that they meet the expectations set out in the national health data governance framework.

These 12 principles set the parameters to encourage greater cross-country harmonisation of data governance frameworks so that more countries can use health data for research, statistics and health care quality improvement.

The Recommendation also recommends that Adherents support trans-border co-operation in the processing of health data for purposes that serve the public interest. It further recommends that Adherents engage with relevant experts and organisations to develop mechanisms that enable the efficient exchange and interoperability of health data.

Finally, it encourages non-governmental organisations to follow the Recommendation when processing personal health data for health-related purposes that serve the public interest and invites non-Adherents to take account and to adhere to the Recommendation.